DIESTERWEGS
NEUSPRACHLICHE
BIBLIOTHEK

Hanif Kureishi

My Son the Fanatic

Study Guide

by
Ingrid Stritzelberger

DIESTERWEG

NEUSPRACHLICHE BIBLIOTHEK

Hanif Kureishi

My Son the Fanatic

Study Guide
by Ingrid Stritzelberger

Picture references:

p. 14: Ingrid Stritzelberger, Denkendorf
p. 20: wikimedia.commons
p. 26: Ingrid Stritzelberger, Denkendorf
p. 29: Ingrid Stritzelberger, Denkendorf
p. 44: Peter Wenzel (1745–1829)
p. 58: Sion Touhig/Corbis
p. 61: © 2005 Getty Images

Druck A ^{2} / Jahr 2015
Alle Drucke der Serie A sind im Unterricht parallel verwendbar.

Redaktion: Jenny Poole, Weinstadt und Ingrid Stritzelberger, Denkendorf
Herstellung: Harald Thumser, Frankfurt
Satz: Stahringer Satz GmbH, Grünberg
Druck und Bindung: Westermann Druck Zwickau GmbH

ISBN 978-3-425-**04966**-3

Table of Contents

Introduction

Hanif Kureishi, born in South London (Bromley) in 1954 to a Pakistani father and an English mother, is a prolific writer of novels, plays, screenplays and nonfictional texts.

His father Rafiushan Kureishi came from a wealthy Madras family, most of whose members moved to Pakistan after Partition in 1947. In Hanif's words (from ***The Carnival of Culture***, 2005): "My father was an Indian Muslim who didn't care for Islam; his childhood hadn't been much improved by a strict schooling and teachers with sticks. Towards the end of his life he preferred Buddhism to Islam, as there was less aggression and punishment in it. ('And altogether less religion', as he put it.) He had also become disillusioned with the political version of Islam, which my father's school friend, Zulfi Bhutto[1] – who the liberal classes thought would become a democratic and secular leader in the new Pakistan – was introducing in Pakistan."

Hanif's exposure to literature in school makes him wonder about the fascination of English writers with the British Empire and colonial ideas. When he reads E. M. Forster and George Orwell, it is clear "that the 'coloured' man is always inferior to the Englishman. He is not worth as much; he never will be. When it comes to character as well as colour, the white man is the gold standard." Even when Orwell, in his essay ***Shooting An Elephant*** (1936) criticises colonialism and analyses how political domination leads to humiliation – on both sides – he mentions people in the bazaars who "would probably spit betel juice" over a woman's dress, and hears "insults hooted after me when I was at a safe distance". The police officer describes himself as "an absurd puppet", surrounded by "sneering yellow faces", by "evil-spirited little beasts" who hate him and "try to make [his] job impossible".

Kureishi is eager to find reading material closer to his own life and experiences. He writes about his longings (***The Word and The Bomb***, 2005):

"Living in the London suburbs with an Indian father and English mother, I wanted to read works set in England, works that might help make sense of my own situation. Racism was real to me; the Empire was not. I liked Colin MacInnes and E. R. Braithwaite, whose *To Sir with Love* so moved me when I read it under the desk at school. But where were the British equivalents of the black American writers: James Baldwin, Richard Wright and Ralph Ellison? Who was noting the profound and permanent alterations to British life which had begun with the Empire and had now, as it were, come home? Oddly, most modern British writers have been reluctant to similarly engage with such subjects at home. Questions of race, immigration, identity, Islam – the whole range of issues which so preoccupy us these days – have been absent from the work of my white contemporaries, even as a new generation of British writers has developed, following the lead of V. S. Naipaul and Salman Rushdie."

In his 1983 essay about ***Commonwealth Literature*** (Students' book, p. 32) Salman Rushdie describes the attempt of the literature business to exclude certain writers by subsuming them under the term of 'Commonwealth writers' as a means to keep writing in English pure, instead of including them as writers of English literature. One wonders if Sir Salman is opposed to being listed as one of the most prominent writers of SAWE[2], together with Arundhati Roy[3], Mohsin Hamid[4], Kiram Desai, Monica Ali, Hanif Kureishi and Vikram Chandra.

1 Zulfi Bhutto: (1928–1979) Pakistani politician and statesman; 4th President of Pakistan (1971–1973); 9th Prime Minister of Pakistan (1973–1977); founder and chairman of the Pakistan People's Party until his execution in 1979.

2 SAWE: South Asian Writers (writing in) English

3 Arundhati Roy: (b. 1961) Indian political activist and writer, **The God of Small Things** (1997)

4 Mohsin Hamid (b. 1971): **The Reluctant Fundamentalist** (2007), lives in London and Lahore

Hanif Kureishi vehemently promotes liberalism and the freedom of the imagination. He defends Sir Salman Rushdie and Rushdie's novel **The Satanic Verses** (1990) in his novel and play **Black Album** (1995, 2009). He is perplexed by British young people who have supported the fatwah against Rushdie. He considers fundamentalism "profoundly wrong, unnecessarily restrictive and frequently cruel" (students' book, p. 39). He draws details from having experienced passionate demagogic Muslim preachers and their captive audiences in mosques in Whitechapel and Shepherd's Bush in the 1990s (until he was bodily thrown out and told never to return). He writes in ***The Carnival of Culture*** (2005): "Sometimes I would be invited to the homes of these young 'fundamentalists'. One of them had a similar background to my own: his mother was English, his father a Muslim, and he'd been brought up in a quiet suburb. Now he was married to a woman from the Yemen who spoke no English. Bringing us tea, she came into the room backwards, and bent over too, out of respect for the men. The men would talk to me of 'going to train' in various places, but they seemed so weedy and polite I couldn't believe they'd want to kill anyone. What did disturb me was this. These men believed they had access to the Truth, as stated in the Koran. There could be no doubt – or even much dispute about moral, social and political problems – because God had the answers. Therefore, for them, to argue with the Truth was like trying to disagree with the facts of geometry. For them the source of all virtue and vice was the pleasure and displeasure of Allah. To be a responsible human being was to submit to this." Kureishi deals with the individual's responsibility in **The Black Album** (1995) where the liberal, atheistic lecturer Brownlow states "People must decide good and evil for themselves", which the fundamentalist leader-figure Riaz counters laughingly "Man is the last person I would trust with such a task."

His own experiences as a mixed-race boy growing up in Britain in the 60s and 70s can be traced in his semi-autobiographical first novel **The Buddha of Suburbia** (1990). His depiction of their family so angered his father – who felt robbed of his dignity – that they did not speak to each other for over a year, and made his sister Yasmin write an open letter to *The Guardian* saying she would not accept their family's history be "fabricated for the entertainment of the public or for Hanif's profit". His search for his identity, his bumming around, his dropping out of Lancaster University after one year, his living at the fringe of the theatre scene, his earning money by writing pornography under pseudonyms, his later resumption of his studies at King's College London and his degree in philosophy – most of this can be found here.

When the first-person narrator Karim talks about his father "Sitting behind Eva and Dad in the car, watching their hands constantly fluttering towards each other, you didn't have to be a genius to see they were a couple. Here before me were two people in love, oh yes. And as Eva drove, Dad didn't take his eyes from her face. This woman I barely knew, Eva, had stolen my father" we can already see Ali from ***My Son the Fanatic*** on the back seat of Parvez's taxi, looking at Bettina.

Kureishi/Karim shows his political attitude and his aversion to being pigeonholed as an Indian in his debut as professional actor.
He is Mowgli in Jeremy Shadwell's production of ***The Jungle Book***.
Covered from head to toe in brown mud, only wearing a loincloth, he is addressed by the producer during rehearsals. "'A word about the accent, Karim. I think it should be an authentic accent.'
'What d'you mean authentic?'
'Where was our Mowgli born?'
'India.'
'Yes. Not Orpington. What accent do they have in India?'
'Indian accents.'
'Ten out of ten.'
'No, Jeremy. Please, no.'
'Karim, you have been cast for authenticity and not for experience.'
I could hardly believe it. Even when I did believe it we discussed it several times, but he wouldn't change his mind." (**The Buddha of Suburbia**, 1990)

Hanif Kureishi explores his main topics of race, nationalism, immigration and sexuality in his first screenplay, which he writes for Stephen Frears' film ***My Beautiful Laundrette*** (1985). A young Pakistani-British man with a disillusioned poet and drunkard of a father works for his uncle to make the uncle's laundrette profitable again. Family scenes are interspersed with business meetings and racist encounters, until Omar meets his school mate Johnnie again who has become a member of the National Front "to belong". Johnnie begins working for Omar and a tender homosexual relationship starts.

Homosexuality in Islam is a controversial topic. In **The Buddha of Suburbia**, Karim's father watches him and is relieved when Karim focusses on Eleonor. "This was a relief to my father, I knew, who was so terrified that I might turn out to be gay that he could never bring himself to mention the matter. In his Muslim mind it was bad enough being a woman; being a man and denying your male sex was perverse and self-destructive, as well as everything else." Ali, in ***My Son the Fanatic***, vehemently attacks Western impurity: "The West was a sink of hypocrites, adulterers, homosexuals, drug users and prostitutes." (p. 21, ll. 10–11)

Hanif Kureishi weaves his experiences, observations, views and attitudes into his short story ***My Son the Fanatic*** (1994, reprinted 1997) presenting us with a disturbed – and disturbing – father-son relationship, in which expectations are thwarted, dreams go wrong and a sense of purpose in life is lost or found – the last assumption being open to discussion.

How to Deal With *My Son the Fanatic*

Not only British society but other western societies are multi-ethnic, multi-racial, and multi-cultural. Students in our classrooms have different religious and political views, backgrounds and experiences. They are teenagers and wonder, worry and think about their future. Most of them still live at home, but they might feel and behave like adults. Some feel misunderstood by their parents and/or the world in general. They might worry about boyfriends/girlfriends, about being accepted, about politics, about society, about their future lives.

They are only slightly younger than Ali, the protagonist in our story. They can see and understand the strained father-son relationship. Thus, reading and discussing ***My Son the Fanatic*** guarantees lively lessons.

The pre-reading phase "Does multicultural Britain work?" gives students some insight into the situation in Britain today (pp. 11–24). By working in groups and presenting their results they hone their language and presentation skills.

In the classroom, the situation of minorities in Britain can be explored e.g. with the help of statistics (pp. 25–28), and additionally in a project work phase. Using the website Movinghere students can present minorities in Britain: why they came, what kind of life they left behind, what they encountered, where and how they live now (p. 70).

It is interesting to have the students reflect on what makes "a good Muslim" and "a good Christian" with the help of the five pillars of Islam and Christian tenets (p. 29).

The film ***East is East*** (Britain 1999, 97 minutes) gives more food for discussion. It depicts an authoritarian Pakistani father, his British wife and their mixed-race children in 1971 (p. 30).

In this context one might want to introduce Hanif Kureishi's biography (students' book, pp. 9–10), and possibly some extracts from his first novel **The Buddha of Suburbia**, published in 1990. The young protagonist Karim, like Kureishi, has a Pakistani father and an English mother. Extracts from Kureishi's ***Rainbow Sign***, in which he reflects about his identity, racism and immigration, can be included here (pp. 79–80).

Before reading the story, students can speculate about its title and present their plots. While reading, they can explore the content of the story with the help of questions (pp. 34-35), and discuss the relevant passages in class.

Additional extracts from the film ***My Son the Fanatic*** (1997, screenplay by Hanif Kureishi) and from Kureishi's play ***Black Album*** (2009) give further understanding of the protagonists. Questions like "What does paradise mean?", "Is Parvez happy?", "Why is accountancy bad?" and "Why has Ali become a fundamentalist?" can be explored by the students. They can write their own play scenes and show their insight and emphasis. (pp. 42-53)

In a test (p. 54) the identity of second-generation immigrants can be discussed in relation to Ali in the short story.

Either in the post-reading phase or in the pre-reading phase after discussing the situation of minorities in Britain (p. 25) one should have a closer look at terrorism, at the perceived terrorist threat and at *jihadi* fighters (pp. 57–68).

The British equivalent of 9/11 – the attacks on the public transport system on 7 July 2005 – can be investigated and introduced by student groups with the help of the worksheet on p. 59. Tapes of the 7/7 bombers can be found on youtube – students will be shocked by the men's calm voices and their bloody message (p. 12).
Explanations of suicide bombers and their motivations can by found in Scott Atran's talk (p. 64), also in the extract from the Indian film ***Kurbaan*** (pp. 65–66)

Prime Minister Cameron's speech, held at the security conference in Munich in 2011 (p. 72), can be compared with BBC's question time where Murray and Mehdi explain their controversial views of multiculturalism (p. 73). In a number of texts national identity can be further explored and discussed.

This will enable students to have a more comprehensive view of fundamentalism, nationalism and identity, and to understand that, as one text explains, "just because we're multicultural doesn't mear we lose our national identity".
These discussions will give the students the chance to reflect on their own 'belonging'.

Pre-reading Activities

Group Work and Presentations – Spotlights on Multicultural Britain

Tasks:

1. Work in groups. Do the tasks for your text, then sum up the content of your text in a sentence or two. Present your text to the others.
2. Discuss and decide whether the text shows that multicultural Britain is a success or a failure.

Spotlights on Multicultural Britain

	Short Title	**Date**	**Content**	**Migration**	
				Success	**Failure**
I	Poll Results PM	2011			
II	Sidique Khan	2005			
III	Lord Bhikku Parekh	2010			
IV	Warning of riot danger	2006			
V	Racism alive in professions	2010			
VI	Qaisra Shahraz	2006			
VII	What makes them British?	2006			
VIII	Revealed	2009			
IX	Sham marriage	2011			
X	David Lammy	2012			
XI	Shafilea's murder	2012			
XII	Ed Miliband: Speak English	2012			

For the teacher:

Students should work in groups. Each group is given one text (pp. 11–24). The results can be summed up in a table (see below).

Spotlights on Multicultural Britain

	Short Title	Date	Content	Migration	
				Success	**Failure**
I	Poll Results PM	2011	The poll results show and the PM states that multicultural Britain has failed.		x
II	Sidique Khan	2005	Last message of one of the London 7/7 terrorist bombers; some facts about him		x
III	Lord Bhikku Parekh	2010	University professor; born in Amalsad in 1935; became a peer of the realm in 2000	x	
IV	Warning of riot danger	2006	This text warns of the danger of race riots, after a high-ranking politician made a disparaging remark about women wearing veils.		x
V	Racism alive in professions	2010	Certain professions are still perceived as racist in their recruitment policy, e.g. banking, politics, law, journalism, and the police.		x
VI	Qaisra Shahraz	2006	Writer, born in Pakistan in 1958; in Britain since 1966, emphasises her multiple identities	x	
VII	What makes them British?	2006	This extract defines Britishness, which now also includes immigrant cultures.	x	
VIII	Revealed	2009	Mixed-race Britain emerges as many couples are mixed. The text suggests that African-Caribbeans will be the first to disappear.	x	
IX	Sham marriage	2011	The marriage ceremony of a mixed race couple is stopped because a sham marriage was suspected.	x	x
X	David Lammy	2012	He is a successful MP but still encounters everyday racism.	x	x
XI	Shafilea's murder	2012	Parents are accused of killing their 17-year-old daughter in an 'honour' killing in 2003.		x
XII	Ed Miliband: Speak English	2012	Ed Miliband promotes the Labour Party's concept of One Nation celebrating diversity and points out how integration is being promoted.	x	

Pre-reading Activities

Worksheet Does Multicultural Britain Work? I

Tasks:

1. Discuss the poll results with your neighbour and present your views.
2. One citizen states his opinion on this poll. Do you agree with him?
3. How does Prime Minister David Cameron see the situation? (Extract)

Poll Results: Do you agree that the concept of 'multiculturalism' has failed in the UK?		
(06-02-2011)	Voters: 217	
Absolutely	161	74.19 %
Rather agree	27	12.44 %
On some points yes, on some points no	20	9.22 %
Multiculturalism has good prospects	5	2.30 %
Multiculturalism is the only solution for the UK	4	1.84 %

Blog entry by Citizen (06-02-2011, 01:40): Just my humble, uneducated opinion but the whole multi-culturism thing as I see it exists, we are a multicultural country. What has been lost is respect and tolerance, on both sides of the fence. People are ultimately selfish and do only what they want for themselves. Community is something that is very rare in the UK.

Extract: PM: Multiculturalism has failed
Press Association, Feb. 5, 2011

David Cameron has declared that multiculturalism has failed in the UK as he called for a "muscular liberalism" that challenges Islamist extremism more forcefully.

In a major speech on tackling the threat of terrorism, the Prime Minister warned that the "hands-off tolerance" of unacceptable practices by non-white communities had only served to encourage extremism.

His intervention angered some Muslim groups and comes as the far-right English Defence League is holding a major demonstration in Luton.

Speaking to a security conference in the German city of Munich, Mr Cameron said that the threat of terrorism must be confronted not only through intelligence and surveillance, but by taking on the ideology of Islamist extremism at home. "Frankly, we need a lot less of the passive tolerance of recent years and much more active, muscular liberalism," the Prime Minister said. While a "passively tolerant" society allows its citizens to do what they like, so long as they do not break the law, a genuinely liberal country "believes in certain values and actively promotes them," Mr Cameron said. "Freedom of speech. Freedom of worship. Democracy. The rule of law. Equal rights, regardless of race, sex or sexuality. This is what defines us as a society. To belong here is to believe these things."

Pre-reading Activities

Worksheet Does Multicultural Britain Work? II

Tasks:

1. Sum up what Sidique Khan said in his final message. What worries Britons most? (Transcript)
2. By using the facts from the extract, write a CV of Mohammad Sidique Khan.

Transcript: Mohammad Sidique, One of the Suicide Bombers

September 1, 2005, Al-Jazeera TV, Qatar

The martyr Mohammad Sidique, one of the knights of the blessed raids on London

Praise be to Allah, blessings and prayers upon his prophet (in Arabic).

I am going to keep this short and to the point because it's all been said before by far more eloquent people than me, and our words have no impact upon you. Therefore I am going to talk to you in a language that you understand. Our words are dead until we give them life with our blood. I am sure by now the media has painted a suitable picture of me. This predictable propaganda machine naturally will try to put a spin on things to suit the government and to scare the masses into conforming to their power and worth-obsessed agendas. I, and thousands like me, have forsaken everything for what we believe. Our driving motivation doesn't come from tangible commodities that this world has to offer. Our religion is Islam – obedience to the one true God, Allah, and following in the footsteps of the final Prophet and Messenger, Muhammad, Allah's blessings and prayers upon him. This is how our ethical stances are dictated. Your democratically elected governments continuously perpetuate atrocities against my people all over the world and your support of them makes you directly responsible, just as I am directly responsible for protecting and avenging my Muslim brothers and sisters.

Extract: Mohammad Sidique Khan

www.globaljihad.net/view_page.asp?id=171

Mohammad Sidique Khan, a UK citizen, was born in Leeds on 10/20/1974 to a family of Pakistani descent. He grew up in Beeston. Then his family moved to Dewsbury, about 30 km south of Leeds. He attended South Leeds High School.

In 2001 Mohammad Sidique Khan married Hasina Patel from Indian Muslim origin that he met in Leeds Metropolitan University as a student of social work. Their daughter Mariam was born in 2004. He regularly attended the Stratford Mosque in Leeds and worked at Dewsbury Primary School with the children of immigrant families who had just arrived in Britain, as "learning mentor" from 2002. He was known as very devoted to his job and did not talk about religion. He used to travel regularly to his relatives in Pakistan.

Mohammad Sidique Khan volunteered also, outside his official job, to work with deprived youth in Leeds in Hamara Youth Access Point – an Islamic charity, partly funded by the UK government.

On the morning of 07/07/2005 Mohammad Sidique Khan drove a car from Leeds to Luton, 30 km north of London, and took the train from Luton to King's Cross station in London. He detonated his explosives at 09:17 near Edgware Road station.

Pre-reading Activities

Worksheet Does Multicultural Britain Work? III

Tasks:

1. Write a CV of Lord Bhikku Parekh from the facts given in the two extracts.
2. Comment on what is mentioned and what is not.

Extract 1: Lord Bhikku Parekh – a political theorist

Bhikku Chotalal Parekh was born in 1935 in Amalsad, Gujarat. His father was a goldsmith with a basic education. Bhikku was admitted to the University of Bombay at the age of 15.
Educated at the Universities of Bombay and London, Lord Bhikku Parekh is a fellow of the Royal Society of Arts and of the Academy of the Learned Societies for Social Sciences and a Professor of Political Philosophy at the University of Westminster. Lord Parekh was chair of the Runnymede Commission on the Future of Multi-Ethnic Britain (1998–2000), whose report, the Future of Multi-Ethnic Britain, was published in 2000. He is vice-chairman of the Gandhi Foundation, a trustee of the Anne Frank Educational Trust, and a member of the National Commission on Equal Opportunity.

His main academic interests include political philosophy, the history of political thought, social theory, ancient and modern Indian political thought, and the philosophy of ethnic relations. His list of publications is long. Professor Parekh is the author of Rethinking Multiculturalism: Cultural Diversity and Political Theory (2000), Gandhi (2001), Colonialism, Tradition and Reform (1999), just to name a few.

Lord Parekh has received many distinguished awards throughout his career. One of them, in 2002, was the Sir Isaiah Berlin Prize for a lifetime contribution to political philosophy by the Political Studies Association. In July 2011, he was awarded an honorary doctorate in of Social Sciences from Nottingham Trent University.

Extract 2: Becoming a Lord

Jane Hughes, The Times Higher Education, 13 October 2000

When Bhikku Parekh was a boy growing up in a small village in India, the House of Lords was a distant place – home to the people who ruled his country. Now Parekh, a professor of political theory at Hull University, is a lord himself.

Parekh, who on Wednesday launched his report The Future of Multi-Ethnic Britain, says he is still getting used to the idea six months after his appointment. "I have been dealing with some very complex emotions," he says. "Many members of the House of Lords ruled over India – some sensibly, some disastrously. I have harboured feelings of gratitude but also of anger and resentment. At the same time, as a colonial native, becoming a lord means a great deal to me."

Parekh's experiences both in an India struggling between the competing concerns of tradition and modernity, and in Britain, where he arrived in 1959, aged 24, have shaped his work. In his latest book Parekh argues the need for society to foster a common sense of belonging by valuing cultural diversity as a source of new ideas, energies and creativity.

Pre-reading Activities

Worksheet Does Multicultural Britain Work? IV

Tasks:

1. What caused politicans to worry about race riots?
2. What do you think of Jack Straw's wish to have unveiled women talk to him?

Extract: **Warning over UK race riot danger**
BBC News, Oct. 22, 2006

The polarised debate over full-face veils could spark race riots in the UK, Trevor Phillips, the head of the Commission for Racial Equality has warned.

Jack Straw, Leader of the House of Commons, has said he preferred women not to wear full-face veils at his surgeries[5] in his constituency because he believed they made communication difficult. It sparked furious debate in the media, along with stories about a Christian British Airways worker wearing a cross and a Muslim teaching assistant wearing a full-face veil in the classroom.

Mr Phillips said the polarised debate over race and religion risked a repeat of the Burnley and Oldham riots, while insisting: "This time the conflict would be much worse – we need to chill." He told BBC One's AM programme people needed to feel as though they were playing a part in society, and issued a warning about allowing communities to separate.

"That is the way to create a country which is not at ease with itself," he told the BBC. On Mr Straw's comments, Mr Phillips told the Sunday Times Muslim leaders had been "overly defensive" in attacking the Blackburn MP. "This was as much a comment about him and his generation as it was about the niqab," he wrote. "It may be that people like Mr Straw have greater difficulty coping with the social gap that not seeing someone's face undoubtedly creates."

5 surgery = constituency surgery: a time when people can meet their Member of Parliament to ask questions and get help

Pre-reading Activities

Worksheet Does Multicultural Britain Work? V

Tasks:

1. In which professions is racism most dominant (or perceived as such)?
2. How do members of minority groups react?

Extract: **Survey finds racism alive in the professions**
Jonathan Parr, Steve Addison, Reuters, June 15, 2010

"Blatant and shocking racism" still exists in parts of the world of work, according to a report on Tuesday.

Ethnic minorities living and working in Britain consider professions including banking, politics, law and journalism, as closed off to them, it said.

"Some professions, especially those that offer the best pay, are still not perceived by a large minority of the country's BAME (Black, Asian and Minority Ethnic) population as genuine career options," said Sandra Kerr, National Director of the Race for Opportunity group.

Called "Aspiration and Frustration", the report looked at the attitudes of 1,500 people from all the main ethnic groups living in the UK, including white Britons.

Business in the Community said the survey showed that despite ethnic minorities having a strong work ethic and high career aspirations, more so than white Britons, many ruled out careers in the professions because of perceptions of racism.

No profession was seen as devoid of racism.

Close to half of all respondents, including white Britons, perceived the police to be a racist profession, rising to 72 percent for Black Caribbeans.

Similarly, over a fifth of Black Caribbeans considered the media and legal industries to be either subtly or overtly racist.

More than a quarter cited politics as another problem area, rising to 20 percent when white respondents were excluded and 39 percent for the Black Caribbean group.

"As well as perceptions of racism, the clear lack of role models and family disapproval, among other things, contributes towards many of the best-paid professions being disregarded by a large majority of the country's ethnic minority population as genuine career options," the survey said.

Kerr added: "The results from the survey show there is still much work to be done, and are a call to action for politicians, employers and educators to look harder at how they can ensure that these professions are seen as truly equal opportunities employers."

Pre-reading Activities

Worksheet Does Multicultural Britain Work? VI

Tasks:

1. How does Qaisra Shahraz[6] define identity?
2. What does she expect of others?
3. Introduce yourself under the heading: “What makes me unique”.

Extract: Being a British Muslim
Qaisra Shahraz, Speech at Linden-Museum Stuttgart, 27 July 2006

What is identity? What do we mean by it?

I believe identity is a package that makes every one of us be a unique human being. Often it comes as a package of multiple identities, as in my case or in the case of most migrants, where we weave in and out of these multiple identities and with such ease without even giving it a thought on a daily basis.

At the heart of it all, I think, is the concept of diversity. We are all different – and differences need to be celebrated and valued, not denigrated or seen as a problem. We are all different in some way or other – even identical twins! It might be the colour of the eyes, our habits, our beliefs, our skin colour, our height, the language we speak, the way we dress, the food we like, the music we love or hate, the accent of our speech – and so on.

Stereotypes arise when we try to pigeonhole people into narrow slots of human behaviour based on our people’s perception. We should view them through the prism of our own world. One’s own identity or background shouldn’t be seen to be in a superior position to the others.

Respect for others’ identities or backgrounds is so crucial, especially at this moment in time. There is a lot of conflict around us. At this moment in time the need to build bridges and to tackle negativity is crucial.

Often this negativity arises out of pure ignorance, lack of awareness and racism. A better understanding of other people’s faiths, customs, cultures and appreciation of their different backgrounds is so important. By doing this we are in a better position to view others with equality, respect and human dignity.

So who am I? How do I describe myself?

I introduce myself as a British Muslim woman of Pakistani origin. Hence I have multiple identities. For me all three identities are of equal importance – all worthy of celebration and all enriching my life.

---

6 Qaisra Shahraz is a British author of short stories (e.g. ***A Pair of Jeans***) and novels (**The Holy Woman, Typhoon**). She was born in Pakistan in 1958 and moved to Britain with her parents when she was eight.

Pre-reading Activities

Worksheet Does Multicultural Britain Work? VII

Tasks:

1. Make a list of the stereotypes of being British.
2. What does being British mean nowadays? Discuss.
3. Make up a list of 10 qualities that define being German.

Extract: What makes them British?
Alan Cowell, The New York Times, February 1, 2006

Every so often, the British like to ask themselves what it is that makes them British.

Is Britishness just a plum-colored passport or is it something else? Is it to do with cricket and warm beer, Buckingham Palace, tolerance and modesty and quaint Morris dancers?

Or should the national image be modified to include binge-drinkers, teenage gangs and soccer hooligans – the standard-bearers of a darker post-industrial Britain?

Is Britishness more to do these days with inner-city grit[7] and people from what was once an empire unsure of their welcome in a land still groping for tolerance?

The lethal London bombings last July, carried out by British-born Muslims, confronted the nation with a stark question of identity: If this multicultural society was to embrace all its disparate[8] strands after decades of immigration from the Caribbean, Africa, Asia and most recently Eastern Europe, what common values should bind a new Britishness transcending faith, race or origin?

Changes have re-contoured Britain's profile. Between 1991 and 2001, when Britain's population increased by 2.2 million to 58 million, more than half of the increase was made up of people born in other countries, according to a recent survey in the Guardian newspaper.

Britishness, redolent[9] of the monarchy, the church, cream-teas and standing politely in line, must now share space with Britishness expressed through the literature of Monica Ali[10] and Zadie Smith[11].

7 grit: (here) determination and courage
8 disparate: so different from each other that they cannot work or blend together
9 redolent: lit. smelling strongly of the thing mentioned
10 Monica Ali: author of **Brick Lane** (2003), of Bangladeshi descent
11 Zadie Smith: author of **White Teeth** (2000), with white and Caribbean ancestors

Worksheet Does Multicultural Britain Work? VIII

Tasks:

1. Why will ethnic groups disappear? Which ones are threatened?
2. Discuss if Britons consider that good or bad news.

Extract: **Revealed: the rise of mixed-race Britain**
Some ethnic groups 'will disappear'
Anushka Asthana and David Smith, The Observer, 18 January 2009

One in 10 children in the UK now lives in a mixed-race family, a major study reveals today, raising future hopes of a non-racist Britain.

Mixed-race relationships are now so common that some ethnic groups – starting with African-Caribbean – will virtually disappear, the research says. Young people are six times more likely to be mixed-race than adults. Experts believe the findings mean that future generations "will not see race in the way we see it".

Lucinda Platt, author of the report and an academic at the Institute of Social and Economic Research at Essex University, describes the shift towards a mixed-race Britain as "dramatic".

Half of all men in Britain who have Caribbean heritage and are in a relationship already have partners of a different race. The same is true of one in five black African men, one in 10 Indian men and two out of five Chinese women. One in five children belongs to an ethnic minority – a far higher proportion than among the adult population.

This week, a decade on from the Macpherson Report into the murder of the black teenager Stephen Lawrence, Trevor Phillips, chair of the Equality and Human Rights Commission will "celebrate" the study's findings, but warn that there is still much to be fought for.

A spokeswoman for the commission warned against complacency. "We need to be alert to tensions within communities that may be exacerbated by economic downturn and to remain vigilant against discrimination and divisiveness – particularly across the boundaries of faith."

Pre-reading Activities

Worksheet Does Multicultural Britain Work? IX

Tasks:

1. Sum up what the police did.
2. Discuss what should be done so that something like this will not occur again.
3. What is the task of the UK Border Agency?

Extract: Police sorry for raiding 'sham marriage'
Henrik Montgomery, AFP, 22 July 2011

Police in Northern Ireland apologised to a couple Friday after officers stormed their wedding and mistakenly arrested them on suspicion of having a "sham marriage" for immigration purposes.

Neil McElwee, 24, and his pregnant bride Yanan Sun, 19, of ethnic Chinese origin, had just arrived at the Guildhall building in Londonderry on Tuesday when eight police came in and detained all 40 of their guests for questioning.

"In front of everyone, our family and our friends, they said the wedding was a sham. I couldn't believe it. I started shouting at them to stop," McElwee told the local newspaper, the Derry Journal.

Sun, who is four months pregnant, said it was not what she imagined for her wedding day. "It was awful, just awful. It should have been such a happy occasion," she told the newspaper.

After being released without charge, the couple decided to go ahead with their marriage on Wednesday.

"The police were full of apologies when they let us go, but apologies won't bring our wedding day back. Apologies won't fix things," McElwee said.

The Police Service of Northern Ireland said they had made five arrests in Londonderry city centre.
"Four people, including the bride and the groom, were released without charge and one woman was detained by the UK Border Agency in relation to her immigration status," police said in a statement.

* * *

About sham marriages:

Earl Aiken, senior criminal investigator for the UK Border Agency, said: "The UK Border Agency is determined to identify marriages that may not be genuine, and where we suspect that may be the case we will investigate. We have specialist teams of immigration officers and police working together to investigate cases and ensuring people are not able to benefit from breaking the UK's immigration laws."
A sham marriage typically happens when a non-European marries somebody from an EU member state to gain long-term residency and the right to work and claim benefits in the UK.

Worksheet Does Multicultural Britain Work? X

Tasks:

1. What does David Lammy say about growing up black in Britain?
2. Where does he perceive racism?
3. What advice does he give to young people?
4. What does he say about multiple identities?

Extracts: **Interview with David Lammy, Labour MP for Tottenham**
Ingrid Stritzelberger, 12 June 2012

IS: David, my students are very interested in knowing more about your youth – growing up in Tottenham in the 70s, about how you decided to become a politician. What made you study law? Could you tell us a bit about it?

DL: Well, when I grew up in Britain in the 1970s and 80s it was a tough time in Britain, it was a tough time to be an ethnic minority in Britain, there was high unemployment and there weren't many role models present in public life. You never saw politicians, black role models on television, for example. And there were riots in the community that I am from, the Tottenham riots in the early 80s. I wanted to be a lawyer as I studied for school. I got an opportunity to go to a Cathedral school, I became a Cathedral chorister at Peterborough Cathedral. You know, I tried to work hard, I had lots of support from teachers and from the Church, from priests. When I decided to be a lawyer, it wasn't easy to become a lawyer. As I said, there weren't any role models and there was still a lot of racism and prejudice in relation to being a young black lawyer. But that's what I did. You know, I always had an interest in politics, I was very political and I was also involved with the Labour Party. And when the member of Parliament for Tottenham died, Bernie Grant, I put my name forward to replace him.

IS: Has race been an issue in your political career?

DL: Well, of course. Racism and prejudice is still a feature of our life, and of course (laughs) it's a feature in my political career. But it is one that is just a fact of life and you overcome, and I don't think that the barriers that confront me are the same as the barriers that confronted my predecessor Bernie Grant in Tottenham, or indeed the sort of barriers that confronted people when they arrived in Britain on the *Windrush* in 1948. For every generation it gets easier, it gets better. But obviously racism and prejudice remains a fact of life and people continue to judge and to employ stereotypes in relation to people of colour.

IS: So even you, in your position as a politician with a lot of prestige, suffer from it?

DL: Well. One, people don't know who I am when I am not wearing a suit and when I am walking down the road. And two, it doesn't matter how high your position, the important thing here is being a minority, and I find myself in meetings all of the time where I am the only black person in the meeting and it doesn't really matter that I am an MP. People happen to make judgements and they have expectations about how bright I am, about what my experience is, all the time. And that is a fact of life.

IS: Young people in your constituency might ask you for advice, because you really advanced, you moved forward. What kind of advice would you give a young man or a young woman from your constituency about how to organise life, how to live life as a minority?

DL: Well, I think you do have to be resilient. Minority status does confer on you a certain strength that you have to develop. You know, there is this myth that we are all sort of born equal. I am not sure that's true. I mean I think that in a sense we in Europe have to determine for ourselves a slightly different path to folks in America, where to be black is not to be a minority, in America, in fact. I think in Europe it is very different, and so you do have to have a degree of resilience and you do have to take your opportunities. It's why it is so important to make the best uses of education and the education system and to fight very hard to educate yourself and your family and to make the very most of education. And there are minorities that are doing that. The Indian minority in Britain has done extremely well, making the best use of education, becoming doctors, accountants, lawyers, not taking for granted that opportunity. So I think that that is important. I think it is important to play by the rules and understand the rules that exist in society, and I think it is important for the government to understand the differences with second- and third-generation immigrants who no longer feel, if you like, Indian or Caribbean or Nigerian or whatever it is they come from. That they are in fact English, or German, or French as well as having some relationship with the country their parents have come from.

So, you know, to a young person, you've got to make the most of it, you've got to be resilient, and you've got to understand that the world is not entirely fair. And for that reason you have to work really, really hard.

IS: You mentioned second- and third-generation immigrants. So as for the idea of identity Would you say they describe themselves as British? Or as Caribbean, or what?

DL: They describe themselves as black British. They are both. You see, in the modern world you are able to have many identities operating at the same time, multiple identities.

IS: And they feel comfortable in their multiple identities?

DL: Oh, they have no choice. That's the way they are.

Pre-reading Activities

Worksheet Does Multicultural Britain Work? XI

Tasks:

1. Sum up what happened to Shafilea.
2. Why was the trial not held until 2012?
3. Do research to find out how the court ruled.

Extract: Shafilea's mother denies killing teen
Associated Press, 19 July 2012

A mother accused of murdering her daughter because she brought shame on the family has denied killing the teenager, a court has heard.

Farzana Ahmed, 49, and her husband Iftikhar, 52, of Liverpool Road, Warrington, are on trial at Chester Crown Court charged with killing their daughter Shafilea, 17, in 2003.

On Thursday, the court heard evidence from Mrs Ahmed who spoke with the aid of an interpreter.

Mukhtar Hussain QC, defending Mrs. Ahmed, asked: "Did you kill Shafilea, your daughter?" Mrs Ahmed, wearing a back head scarf and purple cardigan, responded: "No."

Mr Hussain asked: "Did you play any part in her killing?" Mrs Ahmed said: "No." He added: "Did you see Shafilea being killed?" Mrs Ahmed again replied: "No."

She said the last time she had seen Shafilea was on September 11, 2003. Mr Hussain said: "And who was the last person to see her alive on September 11?" The defendant replied: "My husband."

Mrs Ahmed has always denied murder, but earlier this month the jury of seven men and five women were told she had changed her account and said she witnessed her husband beat Shafilea on the night of the alleged murder.

She also claimed he had threatened to do the same to her and their other children if she ever asked him what had happened to Shafilea.

It was not until last year that Shafilea's younger sister, Alesha Ahmed, provided the "final piece of the puzzle" about her death, the prosecution said, when she disclosed that she witnessed her parents killing Shafilea at the family home. Alesha described how her parents pushed Shafilea onto the settee in their house and she heard her mother say "Just finish it here" as they forced a plastic bag into the teenager's mouth and suffocated her in front of their other children.

The couple allegedly murdered their "Westernised" daughter because they believed her conduct was bringing shame on the family, the prosecution said. Mr and Mrs Ahmed both deny murder.

Pre-reading Activities

Worksheet Does Multicultural Britain Work? XII

Tasks:

1. Which "mistakes" does Ed Miliband concede Labour made?
2. Why is he in favour of a multicultural Britain?
3. What should happen to make a multi-ethnic diverse Britain a success?

Extract: **Ed Miliband: More Britons in publicly funded jobs must speak English**
Andrew Woodcock, Independent, 14 December 2012

Britain needs a "comprehensive strategy for integration" to help cope with the pressures of a multi-ethnic society, Labour leader Ed Miliband will say today.

Mr Miliband will admit that Labour made "mistakes" over eastern European immigration when in power, and failed to tackle the growing problem of segregation along racial and ethnic lines in Britain's cities.

He will vow not to sweep public anxieties over British cultural identity under the carpet, and will unveil new policies designed to promote integration in housing, work and the use of the English language.

Labour would expect migrants to learn English, tackle landlords who pack newcomers to the UK into overcrowded houses and ban recruitment agencies from seeking workers only from particular countries or ethnic groups, he will say.

But in a high-profile speech in London, Mr Miliband will also insist that – far from being seen as a threat, as figures like the blackshirt Oswald Mosley, Enoch Powell and BNP leader Nick Griffin have portrayed it – the multi-ethnic Britain revealed in this week's census and in the summer's Olympic and Paralympic Games is a cause for celebration.

Drawing on his own parents' experience as Jewish refugees from the Holocaust, Mr Miliband will say: "We should celebrate multi-ethnic diverse Britain. We are stronger for it – and I love Britain for it. ... Britain is at its best when it comes together as a nation, not when it stands divided. That's what One Nation is about. But at the same time we know there is anxiety about immigration and what it means for our culture. The answer is not to sweep it under the carpet or fail to talk about it, nor is it to make promises that can't be kept. It is to deal with all of the issues that concern people."

Mr Miliband will accept that there are concerns about the "pace of change" in British life due to immigration, particularly in specific areas which have witnessed high numbers of new arrivals.

"The capacity of our economy to absorb new migrants has outrun the capacity for some of our communities to adapt," he will say. "The last Labour government made mistakes in this regard. We have said we will learn lessons from eastern European migration and ensure maximum transitional controls in future. And we will look at how the Government's immigration cap works in practice. But I believe we can all cope with these pressures if we recognise them and understand how to respond."

He will admit that previous Labour administrations were “overly optimistic” in assuming that integration would happen by itself and people from different racial backgrounds “would learn to get on together … automatically.” Labour did “too little to tackle the realities of segregation in communities that were struggling to cope,” he will say.

Mr Miliband will reject calls for all immigrants to “assimilate” by giving up their heritage, insisting that “people can be proudly, patriotically British without abandoning their cultural roots and distinctiveness.” But he will say that the segregation of communities should also be rejected, warning: “We cannot be comfortable with separation. It blocks opportunities, leaving people at the margins. And it breeds ignorance, suspicion and prejudice.”

Mr Miliband will speak of his pride in Britain’s “tolerant, open-minded society” in which people from across ethnic and cultural divides marry and raise families more successfully than in many other parts of the world. “This week’s census showed that people of mixed race are among the fastest-growing group in the population of our country, a development with which our country is at ease,” he will say.

The goal of an integration strategy should be to “build a new way of living together as one nation, where we overcome division without asking people to lose their sense of themselves – a Britain where people of all backgrounds, all races, all ethnicities, all cultures, can practise their own religion, continue their own customs, but also come together to forge a new and better identity.”

Under his new plans, Labour would put English language teaching for immigrants ahead of funding for translating non-essential information into their mother tongues, he said. Parents of foreign-born children would be required to take responsibility in home-school agreements for them learning English, and the number of public sector jobs for which proficiency in English is mandatory would be increased.

The party would crack down on landlords who cram newcomers to the UK into overcrowded homes and would end the use of tied housing and forced indebtedness which lock migrant workers into atrocious housing conditions.

And Mr Miliband will promise to ban recruitment agencies from advertising only for workers from particular countries and be tougher in enforcing laws designed to eliminate shift patterns which leave people working only with others from the same ethnic background.

“If we work hard and work together, we can build One Nation,” the Labour leader will say. “So that we have a fair nation not an unjust one; a connected nation where everyone has a stake, not a segregated one; a confident nation, not an anxious one. A proper One Nation strategy for integration needs to revolve around issues that are central to people’s lives including language, housing, and the workplace.”

Minorities in the UK

In this part of the pre-reading section a closer look at minorities in the UK will be offered.

Since an important topic of ***My Son the Fanatic*** is Islamist fundamentalism, the focus will be on the life and future of young Muslims in the UK. 7/7 – the suicide bomb attacks in the London underground in 2005 will be a topic as well as what might turn "well integrated young men" into "homegrown terrorists" (see pp. 57–69).

But although these few radical young men are very much in the focus of the media because they represent a threat to British society, a glance at statistics about religion allows us to see that only 3.2 per cent of the population in England and Wales identify themselves as Muslims.

As the FOER report states about immigration and minorities:

The UK is an area of increasing ethnic and religious diversity. Modest migration has always been a feature of the UK, but large-scale migration since the middle of the 20th century has produced a substantial ethnic minority population. In 2001, the majority of people in the UK were White British and Christian but the ethnic minority population accounted for 8 per cent of the population. The ethnic minority population includes many distinct ethnic and religious groups. The original migrants came from different religions including the West Indies, the Indian subcontinent and Africa. Their religious, socio-economic and educational backgrounds differed, as did their economic resources. These differences were reflected in their experiences in the UK, often, but not always, resulting in disadvantages in employment, housing and education.

People from ethnic minority groups tended to be concentrated in specific geographical areas, particularly in London, the Midlands and North West of England. Concentrations of specific ethnic groups were more apparent at small area level than at local authority or regional level. While the White British ethnic group and Christian religious group formed a majority in almost all parts of Britain, there were a few small areas where ethnic minority groups formed the majority of the local population.

Indians formed a majority in some parts of Leicester, as did Pakistanis in some areas within Bradford, Birmingham and Rochdale, and Bangladeshis in some areas within Tower Hamlets and Oldham. In contrast, people from the Chinese and Mixed groups were the most spread out, making up no more than one in ten of the population of any small area.

People from religious minorities also tended to be clustered in relatively small areas: Muslims made up a majority of the population in parts of Birmingham; Hindus formed the majority in some areas of Leicester; Jews made up almost half the population in one part of Salford; and Sikhs made up more than a third of the local population in parts of Ealing and Birmingham.

The tendency of different ethnic and religious groups to concentrate in particular geographic areas has prompted much public debate about the integration of the diverse communities in Great Britain. Research has found that residential concentration can occur for reasons of both positive choice and negative constraint. However, the areas where groups settled have implications for their labour market and housing circurmstances.

The analysis in the Chapter Employment and labour market participation indicates that many ethnic and religious minorities tended to do less well in the labour market than the majority White British and Christian population, although some ethnic and religious groups were exceptions to the pattern. The investigation into the effects of age, qualifications and country of birth show that members of ethnic and religious minority groups were more likely to be outside the labour market, and those within it had a greater risk of unemployment, even when born in the UK and with equivalent age and educational characteristics to the White British and Christian populations. Muslims, those ethnic groups comprised mainly of Muslims, and Black Africans and Black Caribbean men appeared to experience the greatest disadvantage in the labour market.

In London – Photos

Tower Hamlets

Brick Lane Banglatown,
The Central College of London Business and English School

The Mayor of London's invitation to the Eid Festival 2011

Mosque in Brick Lane

Pre-reading Activities

Worksheet Minorities – Statistics

Tasks:

1. Describe, analyse and evaluate Table 1.
   Then write a short report about what these statistics indicate about Scotland.
2. Describe, analyse and evaluate Table 2.
   Write a personal statement by a minority group member in which they state their concerns.

Table 1: Religious identification in the Census in England and Wales, and in Scotland

April 2001 (percentages)

	England and Wales	Scotland[12]	
	Religion	**Religion of upringing**	**Current religion**
Christian	77.7	79.2	68.9
Buddhist	0.3	0.1	0.1
Hindu	1.2	0.1	0.1
Jewish	0.5	0.2	0.1
Muslim	3.2	0.9	0.9
Sikh	0.7	0.1	0.1
Any other religion	0.3	0.2	0.6
No religion	16.1	19.1	29.1
Total (Numbers)	48,031,258	4,639,149	4,783,950

Table 2: Ethnic homogeneity in households: by ethnic groups

April 2001

	England and Wales		
	percentages		All households (Numbers)
	Households with complete homogeneity	Households with broad homogeneity	
White British	97	99	19,336,648
White Irish	53	97	357,289
Other White	57	93	556,180
Mixed	...	45	146,309
Indian	85	90	314,952
Pakistani	85	91	172,510
Bangladeshi	85	91	61,939
Other Asian	60	74	80,748
Black Caribbean	76	83	275,628
Black African	81	86	176,436
Other Black	58	72	31,218
Chinese	81	...	77,384
Other ethnic	60	...	73,234

12 The 2001 Census questions in Scotland were: 'What religion, religious denomination or body were you brought up in?' and 'What religion, religious denomination or body do you belong to?'/from: National Statistics, Focus on Ethnicity and Religion (FOER), 2006

Pre-reading Activities

Worksheet Minorities – Opinions

Tasks:

1. Point out if whiteness is seen as a relevant criterion for national identity in the poll mentioned in this article.
2. In your class, conduct a similar survey. Also state what makes you proud.

Extract: A quarter of English people still think you need to be white
Ian Dunt, politics.co.uk, 22 April 2012

Nearly a quarter of English people still believe that being white is an "important" part of being English, a new survey has revealed.

The number was lower north of the border, where just 13 %[13] of Scots said being white was important to being Scottish.

The YouGov poll for think tank British Future found 52 % of Scots thought having parents who were born in Scotland was an important factor. Being born in Scotland was considered even more important, with 73 % saying it mattered to being Scottish.

"In the years since devolution Scotland and Wales have done more to create a more modern, inclusive pride in being Scottish and Welsh," said British Future director Sunder Katwala.

Thirty-one per cent of Scots said they felt Scottish, not British. Twenty-nine per cent felt equally Scottish and British, 26 % felt more Scottish than British and five per cent more British than Scottish.

Of the English, 18 % felt more English than British and 43 % felt equally English and British.

Asked to rate the things that made them proud to be English, 89 % of respondents mentioned the English language, 85 % mentioned the Lake District, 80 % mentioned the Queen and 86 % mentioned Shakespeare.

The St George's flag continues to have overtones of racism and extremism to some people, according to 24 % of respondents. Fourteen per cent said the same thing about the Union Jack.

13 Divided into age groups: 3 % of the 18-24-year olds think so, rising to 16 % for over-60s.

Pre-reading Activities

Worksheet Beliefs

Tasks:

1. Research and present the five pillars of Islam.
   Taking into account these commandments, present the profile of a 'good' Muslim.
2. What are the main tenets of Christian belief?
   Taking into account these commandments, present the profile of a 'good' Christian.
3. **Discuss:** "Tolerance and acceptance in a democratic, Christian values-oriented system might give room to extremism."
   You can refer to this fact: In Germany, employers, big companies, sometimes even schools have prayer rooms for Muslims and allow them to retire there for their prayers. Not so in Turkey.

Inside a mosque

For the teacher:

ad 1:

The Five Pillars of Islam

Shahada (testimony) expresses monotheism and accepts Muhammad as God's messenger. The translation of the Arabic is: "I profess that there is no god but Allah and Muhammad is the messenger of God."
Salah means daily prayer and consists of five prayers which are said at dawn (Fajr), at noon (Dhuhr), in the afternoon (Asr), at sunset (Maghrib), and in the evening (Isha'a). Ablutions (ritual washing of hands, face and feet) are compulsory before prayer. All prayers are recited facing Mecca.
Zakat or alms-giving is obligatory for all Muslims who are able to do so. They give 2.5 % of their possessions; this is done as a yearly contribution during Ramadan. It is considered a personal responsibility for Muslims to ease the economic hardship of others in their community.
Sawm means fasting and refers to the observance of Ramadan.
The ***Hajj*** is a pilgrimage to the Kaaba in Mecca. Every able-bodied Muslim is obliged to make the pilgrimage to Mecca at least once in their lifetime if they can afford it.

ad 2:

- The Ten Commandments, The Lord's Prayer, The Sermon on the Mount (Matthew 5–7)
- *caritas* (Latin) – charity, love: love of God and love of man, which includes both, love of one's neighbour and love of oneself

Pre-reading Activities

Worksheet *East is East*

Tasks:

1. These are the first two lines of the poem *The Ballad of East and West* (1890) by Rudyard Kipling:

   Oh, East is East, and West is West, and never the twain[14] shall meet.,
   Till Earth and Sky stand presently at God's great Judgment Seat; [...]

   Rephrase them in your own words. Then, with your neighbour, discuss what you expect from a film that uses this quotation as its title.

2. While watching the beginning of the film ***East is East*** (Britain 1999, 97 mins.), take notes to answer the following questions:
   a. Which aspects of Muslim life in Britain in the seventies are shown? Make a list.
   b. Which sides of Roman Catholic Britain are presented?
   c. What might have been the reaction of British Muslims to this film? Why?

3. Compare this presentation of a Pakistani-English family with what Hanif Kureishi states about himself and his family (pp. 78–80).

For the teacher:

Plot summary:

Set in Salford, Lancashire in 1971, fish-and-chip shop owner Zahir "George" Khan expects his family to follow his strict Pakistani Muslim ways. But his children, with an English Roman Catholic mother and having been born and brought up in Britain, increasingly see themselves as British and start to reject their father's rules on dress, food, religion, and living in general.

When in the course of the film Nazir, their oldest son, runs away from an arranged marriage, their youngest son Sajid turns out not to be circumcised and in general the children follow British ways, George's world collapses. He who has placed a lot of emphasis on his dignity, loses the respect of the Muslim community and of his own family. He gets increasingly frustrated, even violent. When his wife Ella labels him as the source of their family's misery and unhappiness, he attacks her physically. The children come to her defence and stop him. He realises that his unjust position has driven his family away from him, that his best intentions have gone wrong and that he is no longer the man of the house. Broken, he goes to the shop.

The film ends on a note of reconciliation with Ella honouring her marriage vows and staying loyal to George – they have tea together.

14 twain: two

Summary of *My Son the Fanatic*

Hanif Kureishi wrote this short story in the 1990s. It was first published in The New Yorker in 1994, then reprinted in Kureishi's collection of short stories, ***Love in a Blue Time*** in 1997.

At the beginning of the story, only the names give hints to the identity of the father and the son. Otherwise it could be any worried father who tries to find out why his son's room gets tidier, why his son's friends do not ring him anymore, why he breaks up with his girlfriend.
But when Parvez finds Ali's possessions in the dustbin – computer disks, videotapes, new books, fashionable clothes – he realises that there is more to Ali's change in behaviour than just spring cleaning or becoming an adult.
He is afraid of Ali's sharp answers, and when he wonders why Ali does not play the guitar any more, Ali tells him brusquely that "there are more important things to be done".

Parvez, a taxi driver who works long hours to pay for Ali's education as an accountant, feels unfairly treated, sleeps badly and seeks solace in the whisky bottle – even during work hours. He is upset. His only aim in life, the one thing that will make him happy is Ali having a good job, marrying the right girl and starting a family. Then "his dreams of doing well in England" will be realised. But Ali behaves in this incomprehensible way.

Though Parvez knows that he has to talk this over with someone who understands him, he does not approach his wife nor his fellow drivers. They are Punjabis like him, they work at night "avoiding their wives" and discuss politics and their problems. But Parvez is too ashamed: he has blamed other fathers for their sons' joining gangs, playing truant and meeting bad girls while boasting about Ali being a model student and sportsman.
When he eventually tells two of his closest friends that he cannot talk to Ali any more although they have been as close as brothers and that Ali gets rid of his possessions his friends explain to him that Ali is certainly financing a drug habit, and that he should supervise him carefully.

He is glad to find Bettina, one of the local prostitutes, waiting for him to give her a ride home, like most nights. Having known each other for three years, they often talk about their lives and their hopes, and they care for each other. When he tells her that he suspects Ali of taking drugs she describes the tell-tale signs to him: dilated pupils, mood changes, sweating.

Parvez starts watching his son constantly. He looks into his eyes, checks his temperature by taking his hand, and goes through his son's room when he is not at home.

He reports to Bettina that he has not found any drug paraphernalia. His son has given up sports, but he is healthy, alert, and steady. Bad-tempered and watchful, Ali returns his father's looks reproachfully – as if his father is wrong. There is only one visible change: Ali is growing a beard.

They drop the drug theory. One night, when Parvez comes home very late because he spent time with Bettina, he finds his wife still awake sewing and hears his son's alarm clock. He watches him and finds out that Ali prays regularly, five times a day.

Since his embarrassing religious education in Lahore - where the *maulvis* tied his hair to a string which was attached to the ceiling to jerk him awake when he fell asleep during Koran studies – Parvez has avoided religion, like most of his fellow taxi drivers. When he tells them of Ali's religious turn they do not comment.

Parvez decides to take a night off work to go out with Ali, to talk to him and to try and understand him. First Ali refuses, but Parvez insists reminding him "that no appointment could be more important than that of a son with his father".

Totally distraught, Parvez tells Bettina the next day what he has gone through at this father-son meeting. Parvez and Bettina are at their favourite place on the moors, where it is peaceful and beautiful.

Parvez is known at the restaurant and is served his usual whisky-and-water while they look at the menu and Parvez gathers his courage to ask Ali about his studies. With a disgusted face Ali rebukes his father for drinking alcohol. Parvez tries to stay patient and explains that he works ten hours per day, does not have much fun and has never been on a holiday. His son stays adamant that alcohol is forbidden, which makes Parvez uncomfortable so he drinks even more. Ali looks at him full of contempt and hatred until Parvez loses his temper and throws a plate on the floor. He is sure that he is not a bad man and needs no-one to tell him what is right and what isn't. But Ali intones monotonously that Parvez has led a wicked life, he eats pork pies, pork sausages, and every morning crispy bacon and on the whole is "too implicated in Western civilisation".

Parvez is shocked because the West is their home, but Ali explains that they are hated by "the Western materialists". Parvez asks Ali for his answer. Fluently and fervently Ali explains that in the future the law of Islam will rule and that the West is a cesspool of sinners who will be extinguished. Ali adds that there has been enough persecution of his people and that there will be *jihad*, he and millions of others will gladly die for the cause and Paradise will be their reward.

Looking out of the window, Parvez checks whether they are still in London. His son sounds as if he is using somebody else's voice. Parvez' eyes fill with tears. Ali urges him to pray beside him and to reform so that he won't go to Hell. They pay and leave.

Ali sits in the back of the taxi; Parvez drives even though he is far too drunk. He wants to know what has influenced Ali. "Living in this country" is his curt answer. Parvez, who loves England because it is liberal, tells Ali so. Ali explaining that this is the main problem makes Parvez lose control over his car. It sways and rips off a lorry's wing mirror.

Back home, when Parvez stumbles and falls getting out of the car, Ali does not help him in the least.

Later he tells his father that he is giving up his studies in accountancy because working in this profession means drinking alcohol, meeting women and also lending money and charging interest. Instead he will work with poor Muslim prisoners who seek purity. Parvez's arguments that he can earn good money as an accountant and that he has been working towards it for years do not impress Ali. He addresses a final question to his father before he retires to bed: why doesn't Parvez have "a beard, or at least a moustache".

Parvez explains to Bettina that he feels as if he has lost his son. He does not want to be treated like a criminal. That is why he is going to tell his son that he can take his prayer mat and leave.

Bettina urges him to have patience saying that many young people are attracted by cults for a while. Parvez sees that she is right – he should be there for his son; but he still thinks his son has been ungrateful.

In the next two weeks, Parvez tries to get closer to his son. He starts growing a beard and tries to talk to Ali about his beliefs. Ali does not compliment him on the beard, he is unfriendly and accuses his father of "grovelling to the whites", stating that he himself is "not inferior", and that the West is not best. Parvez's inquiries about how Ali can judge that as he has never left England are met with contemptuous looks.

Parvez has agreed with Bettina that young people need a philosophy in life, which is why he makes sure there is no alcohol on his breath before talking to his son. He reminds him that people should treat each other with respect, then goes on to say that he does not believe in a hereafter, but that he will live on in him, Ali, and in Ali's children. This speech makes Ali quite upset. And when Parvez says that while on earth one should "make the best of it" and enjoy life, Ali calls enjoyment sin; he cannot enjoy life while their people are oppressed and suffering. He reminds Parvez that "around the world millions and millions of people" share his beliefs and adds aggressively that therefore he cannot be wrong. Parvez does not continue the conversation.

A few evenings later, Parvez and Bettina are in the car together, when Parvez spots his son in the street. Bettina says that he is good-looking, like Parvez, but with a more determined face. She asks Parvez to stop because she wants to talk to Ali.

He does so and Ali gets into the back seat. Suddenly Parvez sees Bettina through his son's eyes – her short skirt, her bright eyeshadows, her rings – and gets nervous. He opens the window to dilute the smell of Bettina's perfume and drives as fast as he can.

Bettina, in her kind and caring way, asks Ali where he has been. Ali's answer is short and impolite. Bettina's inquiries about his studies are countered by Ali even more offensively: he wants to know what gives her the right to ask him questions.

Bettina, with her hand on Parvez's shoulder, tells Ali that his father loves him and is very worried. Ali asks insultingly how his father can love him and have a woman like her touch him. He tells the angry Bettina that he knows her kind. He then asks his father to let him out, but Bettina doesn't wait for that: she jumps out of the moving car, runs away and disappears. Parvez's shouts do not bring her back.

At home Ali withdraws to his room. Parvez cannot concentrate on the paper or a TV programme but drinks steadily. He starts pacing in front of his son's room. When he finally opens the door, Ali is praying and does not turn towards his father.

Parvez kicks him over, drags him up and hits him until Ali's lip is split and his face is bloody. Ali does not defend himself nor fight back, nor is he afraid. The short story ends with Ali asking his father: "So who's the fanatic now?"

While-reading Activities

Worksheet Questions on *My Son the Fanatic*

Tasks:

1. Before reading the first passage, discuss with your neighbour what you expect to read about in a story with this title. Present your ideas. Make drawings of the characters as you see them at the beginning of the story.
2. What does the father notice in Ali's bedroom?
3. What does he notice about Ali's friends?
4. Why does Parvez, the father, not speak to his son about what is worrying him?
5. Which indication about Ali's focus do we get from the remark about his guitar?
6. What did Parvez do for Ali? How does he judge Ali's behaviour now?
7. Make a little sketch of Ali's room now. What does it resemble?
8. Who or what does Parvez turn to for help?
9. Sum up important facts about Parvez's job.
10. What is mentioned about his workmates?
11. What is Parvez's dream for himself and for Ali?
12. What does Parvez tell his friends about his relationship with Ali, and about Ali's behaviour?
13. What is his friends' idea about where Ali's possessions end up? What should Parvez do?
14. Can you see the flaw in their assumption?
15. What do we find out about Bettina? And about Parvez's and Bettina's relationship?
16. What does Parvez do to find out if his son is really a drug addict?
17. What does Parvez observe in his son? Retell what he says to Bettina in direct speech.
18. Can you understand Ali? Give reasons.
    Write a letter – from Ali to his father. He puts it in his room, perhaps behind the cupboard.
19. Which is the only physical difference Parvez has spotted?
20. What does Parvez notice when he comes home very late one night?
21. Describe the relationship between Parvez and his wife.
22. What is Parvez's reason for avoiding all religions?
23. What does Parvez plan to do together with Ali that night? What are his expectations?
24. What is Ali's first reaction to Parvez's invitation? Transform into direct speech, then re-enact this scene.
25. The next day, what mood is Parvez in? Where do he and Bettina go?
26. List in the table what happens during the father-son evening.

List of events	feelings

27. With the help of this filled-in table, turn this flashback scene into a screenplay and act it out.
28. What does Parvez plan to do? Why?
29. What piece of advice does Bettina give him?
30. Point out why "the West is best" reveals a eurocentric attitude.

31. Contrast Parvez's and Ali's philosophies for life. (Add arguments from their conversation in the restaurant.) Summarise their ideas about life in one sentence.

Parvez's philosophy	**Ali's philosophy**
This is a .... attitude.	**This is .... attitude.**

32. Point out where Ali does not obey his own rules.
33. What does Parvez become conscious of when they give Ali a ride in the car? How does he react?
34. How does Bettina treat Ali? How does he react?
35. Why does Ali insult Bettina? How does she react?
36. On whose side is Parvez – on Ali's or on Bettina's?
37. Use three different figurines and re-enact the car scene. Pay special attention to who sides with whom.
38. How does Parvez deal with the situation he is in?
39. What does Parvez then do?
40. How does Ali react?
41. Explain Ali's final sentence.
42. Show that Parvez does not live according to his philosophy either.

While-reading Activities

Worksheet *My Son the Fanatic* – Answers

1. Before reading the first passage, discuss with your neighbour what you expect to read about in a story with this title. Present your ideas. Make drawings of the characters as you see them at the beginning of the story.

There is a parent, a father or a mother, who introduces their son as a fanatic. We might imagine a religious fanatic, probably bearded, with fiery eyes and a turban. Or a sports fanatic.

2. What does the father notice in Ali's bedroom?

It is getting tidier. Instead of a mess, there is now space. He finds computer discs, new books and fashionable clothes, etc., in the rubbish.

3. What does he notice about Ali's friends?

He has split up with his English girlfriend and his former friends no longer come to the house.

4. Why does Parvez, the father, not speak to his son about what is worrying him?

Parvez is slightly afraid of his son who can be quite snappy – when he isn't totally silent.

5. Which indication about Ali's focus do we get from the remark about his guitar?

Ali has more important things to do than playing his guitar.

6. What did Parvez do for Ali? How does he judge Ali's behaviour now?

Parvez worked overtime to pay for Ali's studies as an accountant, to pay for Ali's books, clothes, computer, etc. His father thinks that Ali is eccentric, ungrateful and unjust because Ali throws out all the things he gave him and which he paid for.

7. Make a little sketch of Ali's room now. What does it resemble?

bare walls, empty shelves → like a monk's cell, like a hotel room, like a prison cell, like a room that is no longer lived in

8. Who or what does Parvez turn to for help?

He needs someone sympathetic to discuss Ali's disturbing and worrying behaviour. In the meantime he turns to the whisky bottle, even during his work hours.

9. Sum up important facts about Parvez's job.

He has been a taxidriver for 20 years. He works together with other Punjabis. They prefer night shifts because they earn more money and can avoid their wives.

10. What is mentioned about his workmates?

They are his friends, they talk about everything – from politics to family problems (sons joining gangs, etc.). Nevertheless, he does not mention his troubles with Ali. He is ashamed.

11. What is Parvez's dream for himself and for Ali?

He wants Ali "to get a good job, marry the right girl and start a family". Only then will Parvez be happy because this means he has "arrived", he has achieved his dream of doing well in Britain.

12. What does Parvez tell his friends about his relationship with Ali, and about Ali's behaviour?
He tells them they used to be like brothers, and now they no longer relate to each other. He cannot understand Ali's behaviour. He feels tormented by his son and wonders where his things go.

13. What is his friends' idea about where Ali's possessions end up? What should Parvez do?
They suspect that Ali finances his drug habit by selling his possessions.
Parvez should watch his son closely and be very strict with him. Otherwise his son might go mad, take an overdose or kill somebody.

14. Can you see the flaw in their assumption?
If Ali were selling his stuff for drugs, he would not put new clothes, books and video games into the bin, nor would he say to his father that there were more important things than playing the guitar.

15. What do we find out about Bettina? And about Parvez's and Bettina's relationship?
Bettina is one of the local prostitutes. She waits for Parvez in his car, into which he drunkenly staggers. It is the end of her work night and he will give her a ride home. They have known each other for three years and see each other most nights. He can talk about everything with her and he watches out for her. She talks about her clients and her activities. She cares for Parvez and is interested in Ali.

16. What does Parvez do to find out if his son is really a drug addict?
He watches him, checks his eyes and pupils, also his pulse and temperature.
When Ali is absent he goes through Ali's room in his search for syringes, pills and powders.

17. What does Parvez observe in his son? Retell what he says to Bettina in direct speech.
Parvez: "Ali has given up sports. Nevertheless he seems healthy. His eyes are clear. He does not flinch when I want to look into his eyes. Ali is more alert and steady than usual. But he is sullen, and he is watchful. He looks back at me with quite a bit of criticism, even with reproach.
Now I feel like I am in the wrong, not the boy!"

18. Can you understand Ali? Give reasons.
Ali has noticed that his father monitors his movements and his behaviour. And he must have noticed that his father searches his room regularly and secretly. He is a young man and not a baby. He wants to be treated as an adult.

19. Which is the only physical difference Parvez has spotted?
Ali is growing a beard.

20. What does Parvez notice when he comes home very late one night?
His son has set his alarm, goes to the bathroom and washes, then goes to his room and starts praying.
Parvez realises that his son prays five times a day.

21. Describe the relationship between Parvez and his wife.
He does not treat her as an equal.
His wife is still awake when he comes home: sitting up in bed, sewing. He orders her about although she is just there, not doing anything wrong.

22. What is Parvez's reason for avoiding all religions?
In the Koran school in Lahore, which he attended as a boy, the maulwi tied his hair up and attached it to the ceiling. When he fell asleep, he got jerked awake painfully and embarrassingly. The other taxi-drivers are not interested in religion either and poke fun at the local mullahs who preach how to live but (probably) do not live chaste lives themselves.

23. What does Parvez plan to do together with Ali that night? What are his expectations?
He wants to take Ali out and takes the night off. He wants to talk to Ali and find out more about Ali's life at college. In addition to that, Parvez wants to tell him about their relatives in Pakistan – he wants to show him their Pakistani past and roots.

24. What is Ali's first reaction to Parvez's invitation? Transform into direct speech, then re-enact this scene.

Parvez: I've taken the night off. Let's go out tonight.
Ali: I can't. I have an appointment.
Parvez: No appointment can be more important than that of a son with his father!

25. The next day, what mood is Parvez in? Where do he and Bettina go?
Parvez seems very excited, anxious and in a hurry to tell Bettina what happened. They drive to a spot (which sounds like paradise, with wild deer and horses and a view across the moors) where they often go and where they are happy ("This is the life.")

26. List in the table what happens during the father-son evening.

List of events	Feelings of the protagonists
They study the menu.	
The waiter brings Parvez a whisky-and-water – as he always does.	
Parvez loosens his tie, breaks off a piece of poppadum, takes a drink before starting to ask Ali if he is worried about his upcoming exams.	apprehensive
Ali makes a face and asks his father if he doesn't know that drinking alcohol is forbidden.	disapproving
Parvez manages to restrain himself.	feels rebuked, thinks his son is rude
Parvez explains that he works long hours, has no holidays nor much fun apart from the occasional drink.	patient
Ali insists that it is forbidden to drink alcohol.	adamant, unmoved
Parvez wants some leeway because they are "only human".	asks for understanding
The more Ali makes faces and states that alcohol is forbidden, the faster Parvez empties his glass.	Ali looks disgusted and full of criticism, probably even hatred.
Parvez hurls his plate on the floor.	angry, cannot cope differently: He feels insulted because his son explains to him what is right and what is wrong. He is sure he has lived a good life. However, there are a few things he is ashamed of.
Parvez wants to know from Ali when in his life he has had time to be wicked.	puzzled
Ali points out that Parvez's life has not been good, he has broken lots of rules of the Koran, e.g. Parvez eats pork and orders his wife to make him a bacon sandwich every morning.	accusing, monotonous
Parvez orders more drink.	He is totally surprised, and angry.
Ali becomes alive, leans across the table and explains to Parvez that he is too Westernized.	lively, interested
Parvez points out that they live in Western society.	reasonable

Ali asks his father why he can love Western society since Western materialists hate them.	Parvez chokes – probably shocked
Parvez wants to know Ali's solution/answer.	miserable, unhappy
Ali, speech-like, tells Parvez that the West is corrupt and will be destroyed; Islam will rule the world.	fluent, confident
Parvez looks out of the window.	wondering if he is still in England
Ali says that the persecution of his people has to stop, otherwise there will be *jihad*, and that he, like others, will gladly die for the cause. Their reward will be paradise.	speaks as if he uses somebody else's voice and words
Parvez repeats Ali's words.	He seems shocked.
Parvez has tears in his eyes.	unhappy
Ali implores him to change his habits.	forceful
Parvez inquires what he should do.	clueless, seeking answers
Ali wants his father to pray with him.	commanding voice? imploring voice?
Parvez pays the bill, they leave.	
Parvez is at the end of his tether.	in despair
They get into the taxi,	
Ali sits in the back seat.	distanced
Parvez wants to know if a particular event has turned Ali into what he is now.	curious, trying to understand, afraid of being blamed and being held responsible
Ali says that living in this country influenced him.	
Parvez says he loves Britain because it is permissive and allows freedom and choice.	eulogy to Britain
Ali says that this attitude is at fault.	accusing
Parvez is too drunk to see straight. His car scrapes a lorry and tears off its wing mirror. They do not get stopped by the police.	confused, flustered
When getting out of his car in front of their house, Parvez stumbles and falls into the road. He manages to get on his feet again.	
Ali does not offer him a helping hand.	He has a pitiless look in his eyes.
Ali states that he is giving up his accountancy studies.	matter-of-fact
Parvez wants to know why.	exasperated
Ali says he does not want a Western education because it is against religion, and that accountants meet women, drink alcohol and make a profit from lending money.	sarcastic, nasty, unkind
Parvez points out that accountancy is well-paid and that Ali has put years of preparation into it.	reasonable
Ali only counters that he is going to work with poor Muslims who are imprisoned and who try to live a pure life.	
Ali goes up to bed; he asks his father why he does not grow a beard, or at least a moustache.	accusing
Parvez feels as if he has lost his son.	

27. With the help of this filled-in table, turn this flashback scene into a screenplay and act it out. (individual answers)

28. What does Parvez plan to do? Why?
He wants to tell Ali to take his prayer mat and leave his house. He thinks his son is ungrateful. Parvez does not want to be treated like a criminal or a sinner.

29. What piece of advice does Bettina give him?
She tells him to be patient, and that many young people become attracted to cults, but they often change. Parvez should not give up on Ali.

30. Point out why "the West is best" reveals a eurocentric attitude.
This attitude means that Western (= European) values are superior and that Western people have the right to dominate others because they are better since they are white. These values and ideas were propagated in the Crusades; they filled explorers, settlers and colonisers as well as missionaries with enthusiasm and were especially vivid in the Century of Enlightenment.
What is largely forgotten or overlooked is the fact that other empires existed before the British, Spanish, Dutch, Portuguese, etc., empires.
Among others, the Persian Empire, the Mughal Empire and the Egyptian Empire might be mentioned.
One might want to do research into the Cyrus Cylinder, an ancient object discovered in what is now Iraq. It is about 2,600 years old. King Cyrus the Great of Persia controlled the largest empire in history with people of different traditions, different languages, different ethnicities and, above all, different religions. What he writes in the Cylinder about civil rights and religious freedom gives insight into the very sophisticated civilisation in ancient Persia.

31. Contrast Parvez's and Ali's philosophies for life. (Add arguments from their conversation in the restaurant.) Summarise their ideas about life in one sentence.

Parvez's philosophy	**Ali's philosophy**
People should treat other people with respect, especially children their parents.	(There will be *jihad* if the persecution of Muslims does not stop.)
There is no afterlife. He will live on in his son and his grandchildren.	(There will be paradise as a reward for martyrs.)
He believes that people should enjoy themselves without hurting others.	Enjoyment is "a bottomless pit" – sin. (The West is full of adulterers, hypocrites, homosexuals, drug users and prostitutes.)
He propagates "the beauty of living".	He cannot see the beauty of life when all over the world Muslim people are suppressed.
→ Life is for living.	He aims to achieve real morality which he uses as a synonym for the law of Islam.
(He enjoys the freedom and the choices a Western lifestyle offers.)	(He blames the Western permissive society for his change of heart and says "living in this country" is responsible for his becoming fundamentalist/religious.)
This is a hedonistic attitude.	**This is a fundamentalist /religious attitude**.

32. Point out where Ali does not obey his own rules.
He does not respect his father as he should. He talks in an insulting way and is ungrateful for what his father does for him. He is full of contempt towards his father.

33. What does Parvez become conscious of when they give Ali a ride in the car? How does he react?
He seems to look at Bettina through Ali's eyes. He notices her short skirt and her showy rings and make-up. He opens the window to dilute the scent of Bettina's perfume.

34. How does Bettina treat Ali? How does he react?
She asks friendly questions. Ali does not answer but questions her right to ask him.

35. Why does Ali insult Bettina? How does she react?
Bettina while telling Ali that his father loves him and does everything for him has placed her hand on Parvez's shoulder in an intimate gesture.
Ali sees this and calls her "a woman like you" = a prostitute. She does not want to be spoken to in this way and asks Parvez to let her out. When he does not stop immediately she jumps out of the moving car.

36. On whose side is Parvez – on Ali's or on Bettina's?
He takes Ali home, Ali is his son. But he didn't want Bettina to leave, he stopped and shouted after her, he obviously cares about her. He is caught between the two of them.
Right now, he is alone.

37. Use three different figurines and re-enact the car scene. Pay special attention to who sides with whom.
(Individual answers)

38. How does Parvez deal with the situation he is in?
He cannot do any normal activity like watching TV or reading the paper. He does not speak to his wife because he never speaks to her about his problems.
He just keeps drinking.

39. What does Parvez then do?
He goes to his son's room, kicks him, drags him upright, and hits him again and again until Ali's face is bloody and his lip split.

40. How does Ali react?
First he does not even turn around, he does not hit back, he does not even protect himself, he shows no fear.

41. Explain Ali's final sentence.
He wants to know who the fanatic is now. By saying this he expresses that he sees his father as a fanatic, too. (Discuss: Can Parvez's violent behaviour and *jihad* be compared?)

42. Show that Parvez does not live according to his philosophy either.
He has become aggressive, he hurts his son, he is not tolerant, he does not give his son the freedom to live his own life. He turns to violence to achieve his aim, to propagate his philosophy.

While-reading Activities

Worksheet *My Son the Fanatic* – Turning the story into a play

Tasks:

1. In your teams, decide which scenes you want to show.
2. Re-read the relevant passages of the short story. Write a script. Rehearse your scene(s).
3. After seeing all presentations, discuss if the characters are represented the way you expected them to be.

For the teacher:

The following script was written and performed by a group of year 11 students.

Ali has changed

First Scene:

Ali's at home, he has just come back from the mosque. **Ali** *shouts:* Dad. Dad. I'm back from the mosque. Dad?
His father Parvez is out working, as he always is.
Ali takes the telephone and calls his "girlfriend" Maria.
[... ringing ...]

Maria *(excited as if she has been waiting)*: Ali, darling ... is it you?
Ali *(serious)*: Hello, it's me. We have to talk for a moment.
Maria *(confused/angry)*: You haven't rung me for over three weeks, and didn't get in touch with me at all, and now you just call me as if nothing has happened and want to talk "a bit"? "We have to talk ..." I'm not stupid, Ali, I know what that means.
Ali *(emotionless)*: All right, so it's not that complicated for me. Hmm ... I don't know how to say but ... we can't be together anymore.
Maria *(crying)*: Are you kidding me !? I've been worrying about you for over three weeks now. Then suddenly you call me and all you say is, we can't be together anymore. Why, Ali? Why?

Ali does not answer anymore.

Maria *(screaming)*: I'm so disappointed, Ali! I can't believe it! Don't you dare ring me ag... .

Ali has switched off his phone while Maria was still talking to him. Maria is extremely upset.

Second Scene:

Ali has come from the mosque again. **Ali** *shouts*: Dad. Dad. I'm back from the mosque. Dad?
His father is at work. Ali is sitting in the living room reading the Koran. His guitar teacher Peter calls him. Ali puts down the Koran, and answers the call.

Ali:	Hello?
Peter:	It's me, Peter.
Ali:	I know
Peter *(angry)*:	Ali, it's your guitar lesson. It started 5 minutes ago. Where are you?
Ali *(relaxed)*:	I'm at home…
Peter *(more angry)*:	Good, Ali, very good. But you have to be at my place.
Ali (quiet):	Do I have to? I have to do my prayers, I have to go to the mosque, and I have to find my spiritual dimension. You know what that is, Peter?
Peter *(confused)*:	What are you talking about, Ali?
Ali *(reproachful)*:	I'll tell you. You can't know that. You're a Western citizen, you guys are all the same. You are wrong, Peter, your whole life is wrong, Peter.
Peter *(angry)*:	Have you been taking drugs, Ali?
Ali *(strange)*:	No. I just can't stand you Western guys. You guys changed my father, and not in the right way. I hate you, I hate you.

Ali stops the call, he has to calm down. Peter doesn't know what has happened to him at that moment.

Third Scene:

Ali is at the mosque. Ali's father Parvez, who is slowly getting to know what is happening to Ali right now, is worried about him. He's sitting in Ali's room.
Parvez, who hasn't been in Ali's room for a while, is looking around: all the material things he bought his son are in the bin, computer games, fashionable clothes, all that.
Suddenly Ali walks in. Parvez is drunk as usual.

Ali *(hateful)*:	What are you doing in here?
Parvez *(drunk)*:	Sitting.
Ali:	So go out and sit somewhere else … I don't want any drunk people in my room.
Parvez *(drunk)*:	I'm not drunk, "Aliii".
Ali *(reproachful)*:	You are. You smell like a pub.
Parvez:	But that's the Western lifestyle.
Ali:	So you want to live the Western way, do you?
Parvez:	I want to live in a way you're happy with. But after living the Western lifestyle, it is not that easy to change.
Ali *(emotionless)*:	You don't have to. I'm good with being alone, I don't need you. Trust in Allah is enough for me. I'm going back to Lahore … and you can't do anything to stop me. I'm done with you.

Parvez is crying. Ali starts to gather all his things …

Worksheet *My Son the Fanatic* – Paradise

Tasks:

1. Describe the picture below and discuss your thoughts with your neighbour. Present them.
2. Give examples of where paradise is mentioned in the story and explain them.
3. Sum up the film extract.
   Discuss: Is Britain paradise for Parvez?

In the Garden of Eden

Peter Wenzel (1745–1829)

Extract: **In the Dales**
My Son the Fanatic (Britain 1997, 88 mins.)

Bettina takes a tape from her bag, puts it in the cassette-player and fiddles with it until she finds the piece of music she wants to hear. She listens then, leaning her head back, hums and smokes. Parvez glances at her. He is about to tell her something – but her good mood and company relax him.

BETTINA:	I haven't seen you for a few days.
PARVEZ:	I'm going further and further afield for work, but earning less. They're sacking the drivers who won't work night and day. Sometimes I think – if I hit that tree what difference would it make?
BETTINA:	You wouldn't see that.

As the taxi reaches the top of a hill they are confronted with a view of the dales. But they are looking at one another – with some curiosity.

BETTINA:	Can we walk?
PARVEZ:	Walk?
BETTINA:	In the fresh air. The breeze is lovely. Let me show you a place.
PARVEZ:	Surely there is air everywhere about?

She laughs and gets out of the car. He has no choice but to follow her.

Bettina and Parvez are walking away from the car. Bettina is enjoying herself, but Parvez is uncertain. She approaches a stream. On a far side is a ruin on a hill, surrounded by trees. This is the spot Bettina wanted to show him and, although he is breathless and finding it hard going, its beauty impresses him.

BETTINA:	Well?
PARVEZ:	Yes, it is magnificent. There were places, back home, I used to go. *(He laughs.)* With a girl, actually.

For the teacher:

ad 2:

Parvez and Bettina often drive out to the moors, where, on better days, their view unimpeded for miles except by wild deer and horses, they'd lie back, with their eyes half-closed, saying, "This is the life". (students' book, p. 18, ll. 13–16). This idyllic scene appears like paradise.
Parvez appreciates beauty, he lives in the here and now. He likes being with Bettina with whom he feels at ease.

Ali: "For us, the reward will be in Paradise." (students' book, p. 21, l. 17)
For Ali, Paradise is the place where good Muslims will go. The way he presents his views makes us think of martyrs, of terrorists who kill themselves and others to promote their views (students' book p. 21, ll. 13–14: "My people have taken enough. If the persecution doesn't stop, there will be *jihad*.").

ad 3:

The film extract shows the first time when Bettina and Parvez go their magical place. In this extract, however, we see that Parvez has problems in his job and is worried. Being with Bettina relaxes him and makes him think of home.
Although he defends Britain (e.g. students' book p. 22, ll. 13–14: "But I love England," Parvez said, watching his boy in the rear view mirror. "They let you do almost anything here.") he sees its drawbacks.

While-reading Activities

Worksheet *My Son the Fanatic* – Dreams – Reality

Tasks:

1. Sum up the protagonists' dreams in each of the extracts from the film.
2. Point out if the protagonists behave in the same way as in the short story.

Extract 1: (Not a) Success
My Son the Fanatic (Britain 1997, 88 mins.)

Parvez is with his wife Minoo in their living room. She is massaging his feet.

PARVEZ: Minoo, how has Fizzy done so well?
MINOO: He was always greedy … for things.
PARVEZ: He was a greedy little boy.
MINOO: You are easily made happy and like things to be always the same. That's why you never made a success.
PARVEZ: Not a success?
MINOO: Driving taxi for twenty-five years is not –
PARVEZ: All right.
MINOO: If I'd been given your freedom … think what I would have done …
PARVEZ: What such marvellous stuff then, bloody hell?
MINOO: I would have studied. I would have gone everywhere. And talked … talked.
PARVEZ: Talked – who the hell to?
MINOO: Anyone. And not stood here day after day washing filthy trousers.
PARVEZ: It's easy to say.

She gets up and goes.

Extract 2: Keema and Strawberries
My Son the Fanatic (Britain 1997, 88 mins.)

Parvez has entered his son Farid's room and asks him about his possessions which he has been packing into boxes and carrying out of his room.

PARVEZ: Farid, please, do me the credit here, yaar[15], tell me something! Why make me into the fool?

Minoo is packing the remaining discarded items into another box and generally helping to clear out the room. As Farid passes him, Parvez tries another tone.

Madelaine not coming over tonight? Why not? *(His blood pressure is rising.)* That's what I'm asking here.

Farid shakes his head as he walks past.

PARVEZ: Where are you going?
FARID: To see Asad.
MINOO: I'll get your coat.

---

15 yaar (Indian, Pakistani): my friend

PARVEZ: Playing squash?

Farid shakes his head.

Have you got rid of the racket I bought?

He and Farid look at one another. Pause.

I worked my arse off to pay for that – overtime!

MINOO *(standing at the door):* All the time you shout and swear! That's why no one speaks here! Let him go, you useless –!

PARVEZ: Useless? Who earns the money!

MINOO: I don't know what games you play out there in the mud, but it's practically nothing now –

PARVEZ: Who spends it!

MINOO: There's nothing to spend after all these years! Look at Fizzy. His wife went on a cruise.

PARVEZ: Ex-wife. All you do is send my money to your lazy relatives! – What are they eating there – diamonds?

MINOO: I wish I were with them.

PARVEZ: Go then!

To Farid, desperate to retrieve the subject.

I met Madelaine.

Farid looks at Minoo. The mood changes.

Yes! What about the engagement, and the marriage I am arranging, eh?

FARID: I am intending to marry.

Minoo nods approvingly.

PARVEZ: Yes, Madelaine is so nice. Minoo has written to all three people she knows in Lahore, announcing.

FARID: I have asked trusted people for a suitable girl.

PARVEZ: You go to them secretly when I have handpicked Miss Fingerhut! *(Pause.)* You used to kiss her?

MINOO: Stop!

PARVEZ: Is it wrong to find out if our son is normal, eh?

MINOO: Normal is not perverted like in your mind.

PARVEZ: Keep quiet!

FARID *(intervening)*: You might not have noticed. Madelaine is so different.

PARVEZ: How?

FARID: Can you put keema[16] with strawberries?

Surprised by this, Parvez moves closer to his son who hesitatingly continues.

In the end our cultures … they cannot be mixed.

PARVEZ: Everything is mingling already together, this thing and the other!

FARID: Some of us are wanting something more besides muddle.

PARVEZ: What?

FARID: Belief, purity, belonging to the past. *(Beat[17].)* I won't bring up my children in this country.

PARVEZ: What types are these new friends?

Minoo goes to Parvez. She is trying to get him out of the room.

MINOO: They are not like the bad English stealing and drugging.

PARVEZ: How do *you* know?

MINOO: The mothers tell me.

Parvez looks at them both in exasperation as she ushers him out of the room.

PARVEZ: How long have you known this?

She looks at him.

I am made into ignoramus. Why?

MINOO: He has had many things to take in. What world are you living in? You don't notice us.

---

16 keema: *indisches Lammcurry*

17 beat: short pause

PARVEZ (*devastated*): I am nowhere else. After everything, don't I satisfy you?
MINOO: It is you … never satisfied with what we do.
Minoo looks at him.
A desperate Parvez watches Farid, who has moved towards the door, having picked up the last box.

Extract 3: I miss them

My Son the Fanatic (Britain 1997, 88 mins.)

Parvez and Bettina are in Bettina's flat.
Parvez stands at the door watching her, looking at her hands, face, as she works, hums and sings a little.
PARVEZ: We were only little kids when we came. And the second we stepped from the boat we never stopped working for our families here. Over twenty-five years passed away. I never saw my mother's face again! How I miss them, my parents, and they've been dead all this time! What I would give to see their faces now, for just one minute! But my father was very cruel, and I have tried to love the boy …
Tearfully he turns away.

For the teacher:

Minoo would have loved to be independent, to live her own life: to study, to see places, to voice her views.
In the short story, she does not have a name. She fries bacon for Parvez's breakfast, (p. 20, l. 13), cooks pork sausages (p. 20, l. 17). Like most of the other drivers, Parvez works at night when the pay is better. "They slept during the day, avoiding their wives". When Parvez needs somebody sympathetic to talk to about his problems, he addresses Bettina – not his wife.

Farid, who is called Ali in the short story, is presented in the same way. He defends his Muslim identity and accuses Britain and Western society of being sinful and impure.

Parvez wants to fit in, but he is not happy in Britain. In the film we see earlier that Parvez is unhappy and dissatisfied with his life. In the short story we see him worrying about his son most of the time.

While-reading Activities

Worksheet *My Son the Fanatic* – Endings

Tasks:

1. With your partner, recall the ending of the short story. Discuss what will happen next. Create a final scene and present it.
2. Sum up the three scenes, which are at the end of the film.
3. Point out if the protagonists behave in the same way as in the short story and as in your ending.

Extract 1: Remember
My Son the Fanatic (Britain 1997, 88 mins.)

Parvez, in his taxi, drives along the street beside Farid, who is carrying his suitcases.

PARVEZ: Remember two things. There are many ways of being a good man. And I will be at home. Will you come and see me?

Parvez stops and watches him. Out of the shadows several of Farid's companions emerge, waiting for him.

Parvez watches the boy go.

Extract 2: Self before family
My Son the Fanatic (Britain 1997, 88 mins.)

Minoo is going through her cupboards, sorting her clothes out. Suitcases on the bed.

PARVEZ: What is this?
MINOO: I will see everyone who loves me, my brothers and sisters and all! Come, Papu, I am begging you, husband.
PARVEZ: There is nothing there for me.
MINOO: You are not Prime Minister. They require drivers –
PARVEZ: You can't go home, Minoo. It isn't like that now. This is our home.
MINOO: I hate this dirty place! The men brought us here and then left us alone!
PARVEZ: Oh you make me ashamed, so ashamed. But I have done nothing wrong, I know I haven't.
MINOO: Oh yes, one unforgivable thing.

He looks at her.

MINOO: Put self before family.
PARVEZ: Oh God, yes. The first time! But not the last!
MINOO: Is it because of her that you won't come? Yes, yes.

PARVEZ *(shaking his head)*: Perhaps one day the boy will tire of his moral exertions and will need me. I will wait. You will come home?
MINOO: Do you want me to?
PARVEZ: If you want to.
MINOO: I will then.

Parvez with his head in his hands.

PARVEZ: Otherwise I will come to get you. It is too late now for us to be parted for good.
MINOO: No it is not. I can tell you have lost your feelings for me.

Extract 3: In the woods

My Son the Fanatic (Britain 1997, 88 mins.)

Bettina and Parvez are walking through a wood with some distance between them. She picks up leaves and pieces of tree bark.

PARVEZ: I have managed to destroy everything. I have never felt worse … or better.

CUT TO *Another part of the wood*

BETTINA: Can't we leave?
PARVEZ: Where?
BETTINA: I thought … India. Parvez, a few weeks. You can show me the good places. We can live cheaply, everybody says.
PARVEZ: That's a young people's thing, yaar.
BETTINA: Why have you never been back?
PARVEZ: No time, no money –
BETTINA: Come away. It's a chance. Otherwise … what will we do but the same thing every day!
PARVEZ: You put such ideas in my head!
BETTINA: Good. Good.

She holds him. They kiss.

PARVEZ: What do you want?
BETTINA: More than I've ever had before.

Pause. He looks at her questioningly.

BETTINA: Your face, your hands, you, all of you, you.

While-reading Activities

Worksheet *My Son the Fanatic* – Western Materialism

Tasks:

1. Rephrase the passage. Pretend to be Ali. Use direct speech. In your own words explain to Parvez why you no longer want to be an accountant.
2. Then summarise Tahira's and Chad's words (Extract 2). How do they see accountancy? How does Hat react?

Extract 1: (Not) Becoming an accountant

What had finished Parvez off was the boy's saying he was giving up his studies in accounting. When Parvez had asked why, Ali said sarcastically that it was obvious. "Western education cultivates an anti-religious attitude."

And in the world of accountants it was usual to meet women, drink alcohol, and practise usury.

"But it's well-paid work," Parvez argued. "For years you've been preparing!"

Ali said he was going to begin to work in prisons, with poor Muslims who were struggling to maintain their purity in the face of corruption. (p. 23, ll. 3–13)

Extract 2: The working life of an accountant

Hanif Kureishi, ***The Black Album***, 2005, Act One, Scene 8

The group of students are in a high-rise flat to protect an Asian family against racists. They are armed with meat cleavers and knives.

They finish their drill. Tahira clears a study area for Hat as the guys lounge after the work-out. Shahid looks to slip away but **Chad** *holds him back.*

(to Shahid, watching Tahira at work.) This great sister here, Tahira, she been with us from day one. Riaz like a father to her. Her old man threw her out because she wanted her mum and sisters to cover up.

Tahira: Park yourself here, Hat.

Hat: Ta, Tahira.

He moves to the space Tahira's cleared for him, takes out his books from his duffel bag and starts on his homework. Tahira sits with the others.

Tahira *(to Shahid):* Hat always studying. His father – he's putting too much pressure on him to be an accountant.

Shahid: He's here with us tonight.

Tahira: But the father thinks Hat visiting his auntie in Sunderland today.

Chad: He think we stopping Hat being an accountant. But we ain't. We only say accountants have to meet many women. And shake hands with them. They expected, too, to take alcohol every day and get involved in interest payments. We not sure Hat won't feel left out you know?

Tahira: And you're expected to take drugs in the City. And meet strippers at lunchtime.

While-reading Activities

Worksheet *My Son the Fanatic* – 'Home'

Tasks:

1. Sum up what Hanif Kureishi says about belonging and home in the extracts below.
2. Would you say that Parvez is integrated? Or does he rather belong to the Asians mentioned in Extract 2?
3. Prove, with text references, that Ali is more involved in Western society than he thinks.
4. Show links to the idea of paradise (p. 44) and to people's dreams (p. 46).

Extract 1: Home
Hanif Kureishi, ***Rainbow Sign***, 1986

[...] indeed I know Pakistanis and Indians born and brought up here who consider their position to be the result of a diaspora: they are in exile, awaiting return to a better place, where they belong, where they are welcome. And there this 'belonging' will be total. This will be home, and peace.

It is not difficult to see how much illusion and falsity there is in this view. How much disappointment and unhappiness might be involved in going 'home' only to see the extent to which you have been formed by England and the depth of attachment you feel to the place, despite everything.

It isn't surprising that some people believe in this idea of 'home'. The alternative to believing it is more conflict here; it is more self-hatred; it is the continual struggle against racism; it is the continual adjustment to life in Britain. And blacks in Britain know they have made more than enough adjustments.

Extract 2: Belonging
Hanif Kureishi, ***Why Fanaticism?***, 1997

However, the settling in, with all the compromises and losses that that implies, has been more complicated and taken longer than anyone could imagine. Yet all along it was taken for granted that "belonging", which means, in a sense, not having to notice where you are, and, more importantly, not being seen as different, would happen eventually. Where it hasn't, there is, in the children and grand-children of the great post-war wave of immigrants, considerable anger and disillusionment. With some exceptions, Asians are still at the bottom of the pile; more likely to suffer from unemployment, poor housing, discrimination and ill-health. In a sense it hasn't worked out. The "West" was a dream that didn't come true. But one cannot go home again. One is stuck.

While-reading Activities

Worksheet *My Son the Fanatic* – Fanaticism

Tasks:

1. Sum up how the young Muslim Ali is presented in Hanif Kureishi's article *Why Fanaticism* (students' book, pp. 33–39).
2. Which reasons does Kureishi see for a revival of Muslim fundamentalism?
3. What is the role of colonialism and racism in these young people's lives?
4. Which of the elements does he use to depict Ali in the short story *My Son the Fanatic*?

For the teacher:

ad 1:
Ali adheres to a strict and authoritarian version of Muslim belief. He gives up his own autonomy, his own thoughts and adopts words, ideas and opinions of the *maulvis* and of the Koran. "There is too much freedom", he keeps repeating. He sees the West as too liberal.
He holds a degree and is knowledgeable, intelligent and polite. Though applying for better jobs all the time, he never gets them. His present job is boring and repetitive: he stacks shelves in a supermarket.
He used to go clubbing and had an affair with a married woman. But now he feels strong for having given up these vices, these addictions.
For him, the West is full of crime, homosexuality, poverty, family breakdown, drug and alcohol abuse which are proof that Western freedom and democracy are not working. That is why he will never bring up his children in this society. (p. 36)
Ali is certain that once the existing corrupt rulers of Muslim countries are replaced by "true" Muslims, there will be benign Muslim leaders who will work for the benefit of the people, according to the word of God. In the meantime he dreams of the perfect future. (p. 38)
Kureishi points out that Ali by hating the West also hates his own background, the place where he was born and grew up. (p. 36)

ad 2:
Fundamentalism gives security. There are rules; everything is determined.

ad 3:
When these young Asians' home countries were under colonial rule, their ancestors were considered inferior. Now, in Britain, Asians are still most likely to suffer from unemployment, poor housing, discrimination and ill-health. Their parents' and grandparents' dream of a better life in the West did not come true. But they cannot go "home" – they are stuck (p. 37).
In the short story Ali explains that he is not "inferior" (p. 24, ll. 8–10).

ad 4:
Ali, the protagonist in the short story, complains about the corrupt West which is "a sink of hypocrites, adulterers, homosexuals, drug users and prostitutes" (p. 21, ll. 10–11). He says he has been influenced by "living in this country" (p. 22, l. 12).
Unlike Ali in the article, he promotes *jihad* and will gladly die for the cause. (p. 21, ll. 14–15), he complains about Western materialism (p. 21, l. 2) and evokes the law of Islam, which will rule the world and destroy the infidel (p. 21, ll. 8–9).
He abandons his degree studies because they promote an anti-religious attitude (p. 23, ll. 5–8).

Test Identity

Comment

Content:	10 credits
Language:	15 credits
Total:	**25 credits**

Task:

Write a comment on Ian Fisher's statement; refer to the short story "My Son the Fanatic" by Hanif Kureishi.

"Second-generation immigrants in England are likely to identify themselves as belonging to their family's country of origin." (Ian Fisher, London)

For the teacher:

Extracts from students' papers:

Student 1:

Ian Fisher says that second-generation immigrants in England are likely to identify themselves as belonging to their family's country of origin. I would like to discuss this statement in relation to the short story "My Son the Fanatic" by Hanif Kureishi. The story is about the taxi-driver Parvez who discovers that his son Ali has very radical Islamic views, which he is not able to understand. Although Parvez does not believe in religious values he tries to understand his son, but Ali always tells Parvez what is wrong and what is right, which makes Parvez furious. One night Parvez is drunk and enters his son's room, where he kicks him over and hits him in the face until Ali starts bleeding. The story ends with Ali's question "So who is the fanatic now?"

Ian Fisher's statement says that in England second generation immigrants – like Ali – tend to identify themselves as foreigners, not as British and have a strong relation to their country of origin, Pakistan for example in the story.

If we consider his statement as true, we can keep looking at Ali as a typical second-generation immigrant whose father Parvez immigrated from Pakistan. Indeed, Parvez seems more integrated than Ali. But maybe that is the problem. Parvez tries hard to fit in, he is not proud of his foreign identity and likes Western society because of its freedom. He doesn't believe in Muslim values and even orders his wife, a Muslim woman, to fry bacon for him every morning. His son is torn between these two ideals. He does not feel accepted by Western society and feels better when he is with other Muslims. So he does not really identify himself only with his country of origin, but rather with Islam. He also talks about his "brothers and sisters all over the world", which means Muslims all over the world, not only in Pakistan. So the reason for Ali's rejection of Western society and Western values is mainly because he does not feel totally accepted and feels treated badly by the arrogant Western society which always thinks it is superior, as Ali points out: "The West thinks it's the best." He hates to see his father try to fit in into that society which "hates" them, as Ali thinks. He is searching for a philosophy to live by – which he finds in Islam, explained by fundamentalist imams in his mosque. They teach him about "Muslims that are suppressed everywhere" and that theirs is a belief worthy "to die for".

So maybe it is also Parvez's fault because he doesn't give his son the right message. The message he gives is that their identity is inferior and that they have to try to fit in. Consequently Ali is at odds with a society which sees him as inferior.

I think that Ian Fisher's statement is only partly correct because there are second-generation immigrants who feel fully integrated into Western society and are still proud of their country of origin. In my opinion, parents can influence their children a lot, and if they give them the right message they can identify with both countries and cultures.

Another student:

… It is correct that Ali is a second-generation immigrant, but his reasons are religious ones. Pakistani culture – for him – takes second place. Islam is first.
It is important to know what goes on around Ali.

When we look at Europe then we can say that many people convert to Islam. We can compare these people with Ali, because they did not have any education or a good education in their parents' religion. Most people claim to be religious but do not act accordingly: they do not pray or go to the mosque, for example. And second-generation immigrants, young people, want to find meaning in their lives. And mostly they find it in Islam. And if they find Islam and their families' countries have an Islamic background or are Islamic states, then they feel a connection to these countries.
In my opinion we cannot stop this movement because we live in times when the USA and other countries attack the immigrants' countries. So this is a natural reason for second-generation immigrants and for the generations to come to identify with their home countries.

After Reading *My Son the Fanatic*

After reading ***My Son the Fanatic***, students should gain more insight into the story's topics by dealing with additional texts about terrorism and British identity.

It is interesting to further explore a young man's search for identity and the man's fascination with fundamentalism in Hanif Kureishi's play ***Black Album***[18]. Rewritten in 2009 after his 1995 novel **Black Album**, the play's ending hints at the 7/7 attacks on the London transport system. In the course of the play we can see the young protagonist Shahid between his fundamentalist new friends who support the *fatwa* against Salman Rushdie and his liberal, fun-seeking lecturer Deedee who urges him to think for himself.
More subtle and therefore probably even more convincing than the film ***My Son the Fanatic***, this play allows students to see how a young man can be attracted by radical ideas, by the wish to belong. They can compare him to Ali in our short story, they can also analyse Riaz's persuasive methods of influencing young people and the radical group's ways of dealing with opponents.

Good At Art[19] is a collection of short stories by Farrukh Dhondy who came to Britain as a young man and depicted what he saw in London schools in the 1970s. They make good individual or class reading and help students to understand the time in which Hanif Kureishi grew up, of which he says "to other people you are a Paki, an immigrant, a generic disturber of the white homogeneous environment" (p. 78).

Hanif Kureishi's semi-autobiographical novel **The Buddha of Suburbia** (1990) allows us to understand Hanif Kureishi's youth and formative years better. **The Word And The Bomb** (2005) is a compilation of texts and extracts in which Hanif Kureishi writes about the rising tensions between Islam and the West, the two newest articles written after the 7/7 bombing.

Where do they come from? Why did they come?
Working in groups, students can present British migration history with the help of the website movinghere. They can find out why people from the Caribbean came, what it was like on the *Windrush,* which experiences they had. Or explain the various immigrant streams from Asia. Pictures, personal accounts and facts will give them food for thought and for their presentations (p. 71).

In the following part you can find texts about terrorist attacks and terrorist fears in the U.K. and in the U.S., as well as an approach to understand what motivates suicide bombers (p. 64) and where they come from (p. 57, p. 68).

Britishness, national identity and multiculturalism will be presented with texts from various British politicians and political writers, last but not least in Hanif Kureishi's own words (pp. 72–80).

18 Hanif Kureishi, **The Black Album**, Diesterweg
19 Farrukh Dhondy, **Good At Art**, Diesterweg

Post-reading Activities

Worksheet Terrorism – Fears

Tasks:

1. Sum up the findings of the report on Islamic terrorism offences and how the various experts comment on it.
2. Point out what seems to be the biggest concern and why.
3. Which solutions are pointed out?

Extract: Terrorism in Britain 'mostly home grown', report says
Duncan Gardham, Daily Telegraph, 5 July 2010

Most terrorism in Britain is homegrown, according to the most comprehensive survey of those convicted of offences over the last 10 years.

The Centre for Social Cohesion has compiled profiles of 124 individuals convicted of Islamic terrorism offences since 1999. It found that 69 per cent of offences were perpetrated by individuals holding British nationality. Robin Simcox, co-author of the report, said their aim was to "focus the government's counter-terrorism efforts. There are clear trends emerging with those involving themselves in terrorist activity in the UK. It is crucial that this is recognised and then acted upon by the relevant authorities."

His comments follow private remarks by Assistant Commissioner John Yates, Britain's most senior counter-terrorism officer, that the country faces "eye-watering cuts" in counter-terrorism funding that could hand an advantage to al-Qaeda.

Douglas Murray, Director of the Centre for Social Cohesion, said: "The report proves how great a threat violent Islamism poses to the world – and the fact that Britain is at the centre of this global struggle."

The Social Cohesion report outlines the links individuals had to terrorist groups, their nationality and ethnic origin, their age, hometown, occupation and education, which other radical Islamists they were connected to and what legislation the government used to jail them. The report also shows how Britain's links to violent Islamism are almost two decades old by profiling almost 100 other offences committed abroad since 1993 that are connected to Britain, including terrorist convictions, terrorist training, suicide attacks, and extraditions.

The survey found almost half (46 per cent) of offenders had their origins in south Asia including 28 per cent who had Pakistani heritage – of whom at least 80 per cent were British nationals. Six of the eight major plots in Britain, 75 per cent, contained individual members who had trained in Pakistan and four of the leaders of those plots were directly linked to one or more Pakistani based terrorist groups.

Of those that committed offences, 32 per cent had a direct link to one or more proscribed organisations, most prominently al-Qaeda and the British group al-Muhajiroun. Seven out of Britain's eight major bomb plot cells contained individual members with direct links to al-Qaeda.

The survey found those of Pakistani origin and Bangladeshi origin were most likely to be associated with proscribed organisations.

Just under half (48 per cent) of offences were committed by those living in London, largely in the North East of the city; and outside London the next most common regions were the West Midlands (13 per cent) and Yorkshire (9 per cent).

Nearly a third (31 per cent) had attended university and 10 per cent were still students when they were arrested.

However, 35 per cent were unemployed and living on benefits.

* * *

In Tavistock Square near King's Cross after 7/7 attack

Post-reading Activities

Worksheet Terrorism – Attack on July 7th, 2005

Tasks:

1. Work in groups. Do research on the internet about the terrorist attacks in London, July 7th, 2005.
2. Present your group findings with the help of pictures and the completed table.
3. Discuss what motivated these 4 young men to commit terrorist acts.

Group	**Date/ time**	**Photos/Topics**	**Who? Where? What?**
1	before July 2005	Mohammad Sidique Khan	Mohammad Sidique Khan
2		Shehzad Tanweer	Shehzad Tanweer
3		Germaine Lindsay	Germaine Lindsay
4		Hasib Mir Hussain	Hasib Mir Hussain
5 a)	2003 / 11/2004 – 2/2005	Preparations visits to Pakistan	
5 b)	early 2005	making bombs for the attack	
5 c)	28 June	trial run in Underground	
6 a)	7 July, 7.48	Luton station 4 friends	
6 b)	8.50 – 9.47	4 detonations, destruction, loss of lives	
7	autumn 2005	Sidique Khan, confession video	
8		investigation	
9	2006 onwards	claims for compensation	

For research, use for example
http://news.bbc.co.uk/2/shared/spl/hi/uk/05/london_blasts/investigation/html/bombers.stm

For the teacher:

Group	Date/ time	Photos/Topics	Who? Where? What?
1	before July 2005		Mohammad Sidique Khan, 30, teaching assistant, – married, one daughter – raised in Beeston, Leeds – in his teenage years highly Westernised
2			Shehzad Tanweer, 22, – born in Bradford – lived in the Beeston area, Leeds – very religious, got on well with people, not politically interested
3			Germaine Lindsay, 19, – Jamaican-born British citizen, Huddersfield, West Yorkshire (near the other bombers' homes) – converted to Islam in 2000 – handed out leaflets in support of al-Qaeda, considered a troublemaker – in 2002, married a white convert to Islam, one boy; one daughter born after his death
4			Hasib Mir Hussain, 18, – second generation British citizen of Pakistani origin – from Holbeck, Leeds – a quiet student – went on the Hajj pilgrimage to Mecca – still lived at his parents' home

5 a)	2003 11/2004 – 2/2005	Preparation 1: Pakistan	Sidique Khan spends two weeks in Pakistan Sidique Khan and Shehzad Tanweer fly to Pakistan, probably to attend training camps.
5 b)	early 2005	Preparation 2: bomb making	preparation – the bombs are made in a rented flat in a students' area in Leeds, of readily available, inexpensive materials.
5 c)	28 June	Preparation 3: trial run in Underground	A practice run is carried out by Khan, Lindsay and Tanweer; they are caught on CCTV at King's Cross, Baker Street and Luton.

6 a)	**July 7** 7.48	Luton station 4 friends	They enter the station together, carrying their rucksacks. At King's Cross, Khan and Tanweer board Circle Line trains, Lindsay a Piccadilly line train.
6 b)	8.50 – 9.47	4 detonations, destruction, loss of lives	in the London Underground: – in Edgware Road (Khan) – 7 killed – in Aldgate (Tanweer) – 7 killed – in Russell Square (Lindsay) – 26 killed on a bus: – Tavistock Square (Hussain) – 13 killed

7	autumn 2005	Sidique Khan's confession video	Sidique Khan states his reasons in a pre-recorded video which is released by Al-Jazeera TV station.
8		investigation, search	investigation, search of Sidique Khan's house in Dewsbury, other suspects
9	after 2006	claims for compensation	650 claims; some claims have yet to be settled; more than £11m has been paid in compensation.

ad 1:
The pictures of the young men, which can be found on the internet, show everyday young men from an immigrant background. They look no different from all the young people we can find in our neighbourhood. In his confession video, however, Muhammad Sidique Khan fulfils all our expectations of a fundamentalist terrorist.

ad 3:
According to Muhammad Sidique Khan's confession video, the group was motivated by perceived injustices by the West against Muslims; they willingly gave their lives in the wish to become martyrs for their cause. They perceived violence as the only means to teach the West the seriousness of their intentions.

The desire for martyrdom can be further discussed with the material on pages 64–66.

Still taken from Muhammad Sidique Khan's confession video

Post-reading Activities

Worksheet Terrorism – Plotting "another 9/11"

Tasks:

1. Summarize this short article.
2. Work in groups. Find out as much as possible about "your" person (either Irfan Naseer, or Irfan Khalid, or Ashik Ali). Do additional research on the internet so that you can present them.
3. Discuss if they were integrated. What are the reasons they give for their terrorist plots?

Extract: **Three British Islamists convicted of plotting "another 9/11"**
Estelle Shirbon, Reuters, 21 February 2013

LONDON – Three British Islamists were found guilty on Thursday of plotting a campaign of bombings in crowded areas in an attempt to create what one of them called "another 9/11".

A jury at Woolwich Crown Court in south London convicted Irfan Naseer, 31, Irfan Khalid, 27, and Ashik Ali, 27, of a total of 12 counts of committing acts in preparation for a terrorist attack between December 2010 and September 2011.

The trio were central figures in a plot to blow up eight rucksack bombs in a mass suicide attack as well as detonating bombs on timers in crowded places. Their targets remain unidentified.

"The evidence we put to the court showed the defendants discussing with awe and admiration the attacks of 9/11 and 7/7[20]," said specialist counter-terrorism prosecutor Karen Jones in a statement after the verdict. "These terrorists wanted to do something bigger, speaking of how 7/7 had 'gone a bit wrong'".

The men will be sentenced at a later date. Judge Richard Henriques warned them to expect sentences of life in prison. "You were seeking to recruit a team of somewhere between six and eight suicide bombers along the lines of 7/7 or 9/11."

Prosecutor Brian Altman had described the men to the jury as "jihadists and extremists" who were influenced by a preacher affiliated to al Qaeda. The court heard that Khalid had spoken of causing "another 9/11 as a revenge for everything".

Naseer and Khalid had spent time at training camps in Pakistan where they had learnt how to make bombs, mix poisons and fire guns. Altman told the court they had prepared "martyrdom videos" in anticipation of their suicide campaign.

20 7/7 is the name given to the attacks on the British transport system. In suicide bombings, 4 Islamist militants killed more than 50 people on July 7, 2005.

Post-reading Activities

Worksheet Terrorism – Citizenship

Tasks:

1. Summarise this comment.
2. Point out Hilary Stauffer's attitude/bias. Give proof from the text.
3. Write an answer to her stating your opinion.

Comment: How the government secretly strips Brits of their citizenship

Hilary Stauffer, politics.co.uk, 4 March 2013

Recent reports of the United Kingdom's alarming policy of citizenship-stripping makes for sober reading. The Bureau for Investigative Journalism detailed how over the past two years the home secretary has quietly revoked the citizenship of 16 British citizens (out of a total 21 since 2002), usually while they are abroad in another country.

Those affected are usually suspected of having ties to militant or terrorist groups, and often find themselves suddenly without the protection of a European passport when they are visiting politically inconvenient countries in the Middle East or North Africa. Once they can no longer appeal to a British consular officer for help, these former citizens may find themselves at the mercy of the Djibouti's intelligence services or the CIA's drone pilots. It's a frightening new front in counter-terrorism.

It's perhaps remarkable that the Americans didn't think of it first. However, it seems that even while the US claims the dubious legal authority to kill its citizens by drone anywhere in the wórld, it would be beyond the pale to revoke their US citizenship before doing so.

Thus, at first blush, it seems surprising that the UK – with all its attendant European human rights obligations – would be at the vanguard of this civil libertarian nightmare. And yet it isn't. The UK tends to fight the 'war on terror' by proxy, by making it easy for others – usually the Americans – to carry out the dirty work, and reap the rewards while maintaining the façade of a rights-respecting EU member state.

The gambit of citizenship-stripping is totally in line with this: it removes the final inconvenient diplomatic hurdle to sub-contracting human rights violations to the Americans. Once the British passport has been revoked, it is no longer the UK's problem that the Americans don't play by the rules during interrogations or while on the hunt for militants. No duty of care is extended – so no messy inquiry will be made.

Although citizenship-stripping is morally repugnant and ethically suspect, the Home Office will no doubt hide behind the little-noticed 2002 law that permits such activities in the name of national security – at least until a robust legal challenge is launched. However, the British government's responsibility to its current citizens remains, and this is where they are failing on a massive scale.

The British-Somali community lives in fear: pressured to become MI5 stooges or risk losing their passport. This is not a just choice. Either they can 'inform' (whatever this loosely-defined term means) on the only people who have ever made any effort to help them integrate into their country, or they can be sent back to a lawless war zone where they risk detention, torture or death by drone.

Keeping British citizens safe from terrorism is an admirable goal; enacting draconian policies to put them in harm's way is not. The UK government needs to stop fighting the 'war on terror' by proxy and instead implement creative policies that can maintain security and human rights at the same time.

Hilary Stauffer is deputy director of Reprieve's secret prisons team.

Post-reading Activities

Worksheet Terrorism – Martyrs

Tasks:

Listen to Professor Atran's talk at the London School of Economics. Answer the questions:
1. What seems to motivate suicide bombers? Do their parents support their decision?
2. How does a Hamas representative see *jihad* in Extract 2?
3. What does Farahin say about being a martyr?

Extract: Violent Extremism, Sacred Values, and What it Means to be Human
Transcripts of some passages, Prof. Scott Atran, 9 November 2010
(www.lse.ac.uk/resources/podcasts/publicLecturesAndEvents.htm)

In this lecture about his new book **Talking to the Enemy** *Scott Atran explores answers to this question: Why would someone take their own life through suicide bombing?*

Passage 1:
So the idea of transcendental values, religious values, even in their secular guises, motivates human beings to both their greatest evil and their greatest good. And I think on the world stage right now these notions are competing for the souls of young men and women across the world, especially young men, who have been cast into the driftwood of globalisation. I think the notion of a clash of civilisations is dead wrong. There is a crash of territorial cultures. As globalisation has enabled the access of large chunks of humanity to a better standard of living, so, too, it has fragmented traditional territorial cultures. You know I've spent a lot of time with families of suicide bombers. I have never met a parent who even knew that their child was going to be a suicide bomber. In every example I know it has happened without the knowledge of their parents.
Jihad is the term they themselves use, to describe themselves; they consider it the sixth pillar of Islam. And their willingness to sacrifice is based not so much on a deep understanding of religion. In fact, across the *jihadi* world very few have a traditional religious education.
But if they think their friends and family and community are humiliated, that is a draw to violence and that is especially true here in Western Europe among second- and third-generation immigrants who are attracted to the *jihadi* phenomenon.

Passage 2:
Abu Bakr Ba'asyir (2005): 'There is no nobler life than to die as a martyr for *jihad*. None. The highest deed in Islam is *jihad*. If we commit to *jihad* we can neglect other deeds, even fasting and prayer.' – That's a very heretical view in Islam but it is a common view in the *jihad*.

Passage 3:
And then another event happened in which a young fighter, 17 years old, a Muslim fighter from the militia, in the compact charity group, was killed in a skirmish and Farahin instructed his men to pick him up and started crying and said: 'Why hasn't God allowed me to become a martyr? I've been fighting' – and he has been fighting since the first wave of volunteers against the Soviets in Afghanistan – 'I've been fighting for over twenty years and I'm still not a martyr.' – 'Farahin, you've got six kids, you've got a wife, you love them, and you want to be a martyr?' He says: 'Yes, because there is no nobler thing in life than to die for a cause as a martyr with your friends.'

Post-reading Activities

Worksheet *Kurbaan*
(India 2009, 180 minutes)

Tasks:

1. Sum up Ehsaan Khan's opinions in the extract.
2. Write a sequel to the extract below.
3. Find a review of *Kurbaan* (India 2009, 180 minutes) and summarise it.
4. In what ways is this film not a typical Bollywood production?

Extract: Islam explained
Kurbaan, India 2009, 180 min.

Ehsaan Khan is a professor at Mumbai University. He meets Hindu lecturer Avantika Ahuja, who has returned to Delhi because of her father's illness. They fall in love, get married and go to the US together. Ehsaan is appointed as a professor and teaches Islam and the Modern World at the same university as Avantika. In this scene, Ehsaan is teaching in a lecture hall full of mainly US students when Riyaz, a foreign-looking student, comes in and joins the talk about jihad.

Ehsaan: The word 'jihad' is mentioned in the Koran about 41 times. The words mercy, peace and compassion are mentioned about 255 times.
(A knock on the door) Yes, come in.
(Riyaz enters) Come on in, Riyaz. Sit down, please.

Ehsaan: Contrary to popular belief in most western cultures, Islam *is* a religion that preaches peace and tolerance.

Patricia puts her hand up.

Ehsaan: Yes, Patricia?

Patricia: If Islam is really a religion that preaches peace, then how come that the world's most troubled spots are the West Bank, Afghanistan, Pakistan, Iraq. They are all plagued with Islamic terrorism.

Ehsaan: That depends on your definition of terrorism. Some might argue that the U.S. invasions of countries like Iraq and Pakistan are also acts of terrorism.

Patricia: Those were acts of war to get rid of despotic regimes.

Ehsaan: Or means at getting at the countries' oil.

Male student 1: Conspiracy theories.

Ehsaan, looking at Riyaz: Yes, please, go ahead.

Riyaz: Mr Khan is right. I mean, if we are talking about terrorists: the world's biggest terrorists are the white superpowers.

Male student 2: Come on now.

Riyaz: Oh, really. Stop and think about it.

Patricia: Explain 9/11.

Riyaz: Okay. *(pause)* Do you know how many people died in the twin tower strike?

Patricia: Around 3,000.

Riyaz: And do you have any idea how many people died in the bombing of Afghanistan? Take a wild guess. *(pause)* More than 15,000 people died – and that's just conservative figures. About 50,000 tons of explosives were dropped on innocent civilians. Men, women, children.

Patricia: But that was because of the Taliban.

Riyaz: Now that you brought it up. Did you know that the Taliban was a creation of the CIA? To fight the Russians!

Student 1: Whatever. They were still harbouring terrorists.

Riyaz: Yeah, right. Terrorists that were never found. Just like the weapons of mass destruction that were never found in Iraq. Do you want to know about the death toll in Iraq? 500,000 civilians – and counting. And what do Britain and America say when they don't find these weapons? It's simple. They just say 'Sorry'. And still refuse to relinquish control of these countries.

Student 3: What are you trying to say?

Riyaz: What I am trying to say is that just because you are American, wear a fancy suit and call yourself the president doesn't make you any less of a terrorist. I'm saying if you don't stop meddling in other people's countries you will face a backlash.

Patricia: If Muslims like you feel that way, why don't you get out of our country?

Riyaz: *(after a long pause)* We will. As soon as you promise to leave ours.

Post-reading Activities

Worksheet Terrorism – "Open Source *Jihad*"

Tasks:

1. Work in pairs. One partner works with Text 1, the other with Text 2.
   List the most important facts, then present your text to your neighbour.
2. Write a summary combining the two texts.

Text 1: Al Qaeda issues English-language advice magazine for militants

Angus McDowall, Andrew Roche, Reuters, 2 March 2013

Riyadh – Al Qaeda in the Arabian Peninsula (AQAP), the Islamist movement's most active branch, has released an English-language magazine advising would-be militants on how to torch parked cars and cause traffic accidents.

AQAP, based in the impoverished, lawless state of Yemen, has previously plotted to bring down international airlines and is seen by Western governments as a danger to oil-producing Gulf states and major crude shipment routes.

In a section entitled "open source *jihad*", the magazine gives tips on how to set fire to parked cars, including advice such as "don't get petrol on yourself", and suggests spilling oil on road bends to cause crashes.

An editorial in the magazine warned France to end its military intervention in Mali, citing the U.S. experiences in Afghanistan and Iraq, which it said made "them bite their fingertips in regret".

The magazine also called on militants to attack 11 public figures in the West, including author Salman Rushdie – whose 1988 novel The Satanic Verses was seen by many Muslims as blasphemous. It says they are "wanted dead or alive for crimes against Islam". Among others are Dutch politician Geert Wilders and Canadian-Somalian activist Ayaan Hirsi Ali, both strong critics of Islam, and U.S. pastor Terry Jones, who staged a public burning of copies of the Koran.

Text 2: Al Qaeda in Yemen post online English magazine calling for holy war

AP, 1 March 2013

Cairo – Yemen's al Qaeda in the Arabian Peninsula – considered to be the terror network's most dangerous branch – is urging for holy war in a new edition of its online English-language magazine. The edition appeared on militant websites Thursday after an almost nine month interval.

The magazine's former editor, American Samir Khan, was killed in a U.S. drone strike in September 2011 in Yemen, together with the U.S.-born militant cleric Anwar al-Awlaki.
The magazine's new editor, Yahia Ibrahim, praised the two slain al Qaeda figures as a "team whose martyrdom inspires" others.

The new edition includes excerpts from an interview with al Qaeda's American spokesman, Adam Gadahn, who uses the name "Azzam the American". He urges militants to continue fighting America and other NATO members to destroy them economically and militarily.

Post-reading Activities

Worksheet Terrorism – Homegrown Terrorists

Tasks:

1. What does this new report focus on?
2. Present the profile of an al Qaeda recruit.
3. Do research on the bombers of the Boston Marathon, 15 April 2013, and present your findings.

Extract: America's Homegrown Terrorists
Eli Lake, The Daily Beast, 26 February 2013

In 1997, a Sudanese man named Jamal Ahmed al-Fadl became the first person to plead guilty in the United States to offenses related to being part of al Qaeda. Between al-Fadl's conviction and the end of 2011, 170 other individuals have been convicted by American courts or military commissions for committing crimes on behalf of, or inspired by, the organization responsible for the 9-11 attacks.

A new study finds that a majority of these operatives were American citizens. Nearly a quarter were converts to Islam. More than half had completed some form of college course work.

While several organizations have examined the trend of Americans joining al Qaeda, the new study from the Henry Jackson Society, a right-leaning think tank in London, goes into specific biographical and demographic detail on the individuals themselves.

As for who joins al Qaeda, the report says there aren't many advance signs. "There needs to be an acknowledgement that the threat can come from any region of the country, from any background or educational status," said the report's main author, Robin Simcox. "There is no classic profile for the home grown al Qaeda threat in the United States, the key here is to look at the spread of ideology and not profile for education, race or social status."

Mike Hayden, the last CIA director under George W. Bush and the author of the preface to the new study, compared it to a baseball encyclopedia. "The way I would view this, this is not about targeting Americans or American groups, this is about being aware that Americans and American groups are being targeted by al Qaeda for recruitment," he said.

This is a very different picture of the al Qaeda threat top national security officials warned about after 9-11. In that world, the threat was largely from highly trained individuals who infiltrated into the US on fake passports or through other means. The report found that only 47 percent of the individuals convicted of al Qaeda-reladed offenses attended some kind of training camp. Of those who received training, 68 percent attended a camp in Afghanistan, 29 percent in Pakistan and 5 percent in Somalia.

Of the 171 convicted, 51 were born in the US. Of those, 17 are African American and 13 are Caucasian. The rest include Iraqi-, Jordanian-, and Egyptian-Americans. The study also shows that 89 of 171 individuals convicted have received at least some kind of college education, with 39 individuals earning an advanced degree. At the time of their arrests, 97 of the total either had jobs or were in school.

Al Qaeda-related offenses, as defined by the study, can include anything from providing material support to al Qaeda to participating in attempted mass murder.

Post-reading Activities

Worksheet Terrorism – A Terrorist Threat

Tasks:

1. Before looking at the text, discuss with your neighbour how to describe a person who might be considered a "terrorist threat". Present your ideas to the class.
2. Sum up this news.
3. Point out the mindset behind the accusation.

Pa. kindergartner suspended for bubble gun remark

Associated Press, 19 January 2013

MOUNT CARMEL, Pa. – A 5-year-old Pennsylvania girl who told another girl she was going to shoot her with a pink toy gun that blows soapy bubbles has been suspended from kindergarten.

Her family has hired an attorney to fight the punishment, which initially was 10 days but was reduced to two.

Attorney Robin Ficker says Mount Carmel Area School District officials labeled the girl a "terrorist threat" for the bubble gun remark, made Jan. 10 as both girls waited for a school bus.

Ficker says the girl didn't even have the bubble gun with her and has never fired a real gun. He says she's "the least terroristic person in Pennsylvania".

School district solicitor Edward Greco tells pennlive.com that officials are looking into the case. He said Friday school officials aren't at liberty to discuss disciplinary actions.

For the teacher:

ad 3:

It is difficult for Germans to understand the school district's policy ("zero tolerance") and to follow the lawyer's argumentation that she "has never fired a real gun". In most European countries that is considered normal.

In the U.S., however, guns have a different status. For example, the firearms company Crickett offers a whole range of guns for children, and they proudly display photos of small children with their guns on their website's kids' corner.

And that is why one can find headlines like this one, from May 1st, 2013: "5-year-old boy shots 2-year old sister in Kentucky." In this tragic accident a five-year old boy shot his two-year-old sister with the gun he had been given for his birthday the previous year. The parents had mistakenly assumed that the gun he was playing with was unloaded.

"Terrorist" accusations, on the other hand, are taken so seriously that a child who nibbled his strawberry Danish pastry into a gunlike shape and pointed it at another child in the school cafeteria, was excluded from school. (The child is Josh Welch from Maryland. The incident happened in March 2013.)

One Way of Countering Terrorism

Content:	10 credits
Language:	15 credits
Total:	**25 credits**

Task:

Explain to an English friend what HATIF is and how HATIF can offer a way out of Islamic fanaticism.

Text: **Heraus aus Terrorismus und islamistischem Fanatismus – HATIF!**
Bundesamt für Verfassungsschutz
htpp://www.verfassungsschutz.de/de/arbeitsfelder/af_islamismus/hatif_de.html

Das friedliche Zusammenleben von Menschen unterschiedlicher Herkunft und Religion ist unverzichtbare Grundlage des Lebens in Deutschland. Individuelle und organisierte Gewalt als Mittel zur Durchsetzung von Zielen kann nicht akzeptiert werden, egal wie sie ideologisch oder religiös begründet wird. Der Anwendung und Befürwortung von Gewalt ist eine klare Absage zu erteilen. Aus diesem Grund möchte das Bundesamt für Verfassungsschutz einen Beitrag zum Maßnahmenkatalog der Bundesregierung gegen Extremismus und Gewalt leisten und will mit dem Programm HATIF Unterstützung anbieten.
HATIF steht für: Heraus Aus Terrorismus und Islamistischem Fanatismus

Was ist HATIF?
HATIF ist ein Programm des Bundesamtes für Verfassungsschutz, das Menschen helfen möchte, sich aus einem Umfeld zu lösen, in dem ein fanatischer, die Anwendung von Gewalt befürwortender Islam gepredigt und gelebt wird.
Fachkräfte im Bundesamt für Verfassungsschutz begleiten diese Loslösung durch ein individuelles Angebot an Beratung und Betreuung. Das Bundesamt für Verfassungsschutz kooperiert dabei bundesweit mit staatlichen Trägern von Hilfsangeboten.
Die Hotline steht seit dem 19. Juli 2010 zur Verfügung.

Wen will HATIF erreichen?
HATIF richtet sich an Menschen, die in den Einflussbereich von fanatischen islamistischen oder islamistisch-terroristischen Gruppierungen geraten sind, sich daraus lösen wollen und das aus eigener Kraft nicht schaffen, sowie deren Eltern, Familienangehörige und Freunde.

Was bietet HATIF?
Persönliche Betreuung durch Gespräche, Hilfe bei Behördenkontakten, Unterstützung bei Bedrohung durch Angehörige und Unterstützer der islamistischen terroristischen Szene, Vermittlung von schulischen oder beruflichen Qualifizierungsmaßnahmen, materielle Hilfe im Einzelfall bei zwingend erforderlichen Maßnahmen.
Auf Wunsch vermittelt HATIF auch externe Hilfs- und Unterstüzungsangebote. HATIF ist telefonisch rund um die Uhr erreichbar. Auch eine türkisch- bzw. arabischsprachige Betreuung ist möglich. Allen Anrufern sichert das Bundesamt für Verfassungsschutz absolute Vertraulichkeit zu.

Telefon: + 49 (0) 221 - 792 - 6999

Post-reading Activities

Worksheet Migration History – Project Work

Tasks:

Group work

1. From the Migration history gallery's website www.movinghere.org.uk choose one community of immigrants you want to focus on. Divide up tasks (timeline, photos, examples, areas ...). You can use the following questions:
   What was it like in the country of origin and why did people choose to move to England?
   What was the journey like?
   What were the people's experiences of arriving and settling in England?
   How do people reconnect with their (or their parents') countries of origin?
2. Prepare a powerpoint presentation.
3. Take notes during the others' presentations.
4. Discuss similarities and differences in migration patterns.

Extract: Moving here
www.movinghere.org.uk

People have been coming to Britain from other countries for thousands of years. Some have stayed for only a short while, going back home or moving on. Others have made homes here. Those that settle are called immigrants.

The history of migration into Britain is like a tapestry that tells a rich and exciting story, with interwoven threads of bright, contrasting, sometimes clashing colours.

The story is not without hardship. There have often been difficult journeys to get here, leaving family and friends behind. Some of those who have settled came as refugees, driven from their homes by natural disasters, persecution or war. From time to time they may have encountered prejudice and discrimination but have gone on to settle and establish communities.

Over the centuries immigrants have influenced every aspect of life in Britain from clothes, food and language, to religion and politics.

Collected together here for the first time are documents, photographs, sound and film clips selected by curators and researchers at archives and museums all over England. These incredible fragments of history are presented by specialist writers and historians and available for you to download.

Post-reading Activities

Worksheet National Identity I

Tasks:

1. What kind of picture does PM David Cameron draw of the Muslim community in Britain today?
2. Point out PM Cameron's attitude towards the Muslim community in Britain by stating and explaining the examples he uses.
3. What might be criticised by Muslims?
4. Why does he make a speech like that?

Extract: Something to Belong To, Something to Believe In
PM's speech at Munich Security Conference, 5 February 2011

[...] In the UK, some young men find it hard to identify with the traditional Islam practised at home by their parents, whose customs can seem staid[21] when transplanted to modern Western countries. But these young men find it hard to identify with Britain, too, because we have allowed the weakening of our collective identity. Under the doctrine of state multiculturalism, we have encouraged different cultures to live separate lives, apart from each other and apart from the mainstream. We've failed to provide a vision of society to which they feel they want to belong. We've even tolerated these segregated communities behaving in ways that run completely counter to our values.

So, when a white person holds objectionable views, racist views for example, we rightly condemn them. But when equally unacceptable views or practices come from someone who isn't white, we've been too cautious frankly – frankly, even fearful – to stand up to them. The failure, for instance of some to confront the horrors of forced marriage, the practice where some young girls are bullied and sometimes taken abroad to marry someone when they don't want to, is a case in point. This hands-off tolerance has only served to reinforce the sense that not enough is shared. And this all leaves some young Muslims feeling rootless. And the search for something to belong to and something to believe in can lead them to this extremist ideology. Now for sure, they don't turn into terrorists overnight, but what we see – and what we see in so many European countries – is a process of radicalisation.

Internet chatrooms are virtual meeting places where attitudes are shared, strengthened and validated. In some mosques, preachers of hate can sow misinformation about the plight of Muslims elsewhere. In our communities, groups and organisations led by young, dynamic leaders promote separatism by encouraging Muslims to define themselves solely in terms of their religion. All these interactions can engender a sense of community, a substitute for what the wider society has failed to supply. [...]

21 staid: boring and old-fashioned

Post-reading Activities

Worksheet National Identity II

Tasks:

1. View the tape. How does Douglas Murray define multiculturalism?
2. What does Mehdi Hassan explain?

Douglas Murray: Multiculturalism in Britain is 'divisive'

http://news.bbc.co.uk/2/hi/programmes/question_time/9394168.stm
11 February 2011

Neo-conservative author and the director for the centre of social cohesion, Douglas Murray, says multiculturalism in Britain is "divisive" and has created a society with "different values for different people".

The New Statesman's Mehdi Hassan responded to Mr Murray's comments claiming that multiculturalism in Britain had been a success.

Earlier this week the Prime Minister David Cameron made a speech in which he said he wanted to see the end of "state multiculturalism".

Watch more on the Question Time website.

Transcript/Extract:

Interviewer: Do you agree with David Cameron that multiculturalism in the UK has failed?

Murray: Yes, I think he was right. And I think we should start with just reminding us of what multiculturalism is not. Multiculturalism is not multiracialism, it isn't pluralism.
For years, the multicultural policy has been able to glide along in part because of that misunderstanding. Because of the misunderstanding that when you talk about multiculturalism as a policy what you are talking about is solely immigration, or multiracialism and so on
It's allowed itself an incredibly easy ride not least by the fact that this confusion has meant that any criticism of multiculturalism has been immediately decried for years now as racist.

Interviewer: What do you understand by multiculturalism?

Murray: Multiculturalism as a policy is the following: It is the idea that there is such a thing as British society or British culture. There are simply different communities which you are born into. If for instance you are born into a community of an Asian background you will be treated by Government throughout your life as a member of the Asian community. If you are born into some other racial or religious grouping you will be regarded in that way. And that anything in that group could be different from what the normal society goes on. Let me give you one quick example. It has been quite commonly known in recent years that girls of Pakistani origin have at the age of sixteen been taken out of British schools and married to older men.

Listen to the rest of the interview on http://news.bbc.co.uk/2/hi/programmes/question_time/9394168.stm

Post-reading Activities

Worksheet National Identity III

Tasks:

1. Sum up what Varun Uberoi and Taruq Modood state about identity.
2. Point out the differences to PM Cameron's opinion.

Comment: Just because we're multicultural doesn't mean we lose our national identity

www.politics.co.uk, Varun Uberoi & Tariq Modood, 14 November 2012

Last year in Munich David Cameron criticised 'state multiculturalism' and endorsed nationhood. Doing so is common and as Ed Milliband emphasises both 'one nation' and the cost of immigration, he may end up doing this too.

Multiculturalism allegedly causes people to focus on minority identities not national ones, prevents the state promoting a national culture or reduces what citizens share to such an extent that they no longer possess one. Those making such claims seldom define multiculturalism, national identities or national culture or explain why they see these ideas in the way that they do. What these ideas denote and their conceptual, logical and other relationships to one another are not self-evident.

We try to avoid some of these difficulties by first explaining how multiculturalists see the relationship between policies of multiculturalism and nationhood so as to identify a multiculturalist goal in relation to what is often called 'Britishness'.

Multiculturalists argue that cultural diversity is in-eliminable without an unacceptable level of coercion and is a source of intercultural learning. But hostility, competition and conflict between cultural groups will make such diversity seem divisive, destabilising and necessary to subdue. A nation's identity thus becomes important as it is the institutions, laws, history, traditions and other features that make the nation what it is; and related to the latter are people's sense of their nation's identity, or their national identities which enables them to feel that regardless of differences in class, region, religion and so on that they share institutions, laws, history and traditions and are thus, inter alia, a group. This helps them to take collective action, forge collective goals and accept collectively binding decisions.

However, the cultural majority often see the nation as only theirs and this exacerbates the exclusion and discrimination of cultural minorities. Policies of multiculturalism, however, help to make a nation's identity more inclusive. Hence anti-discrimination measures or legal exemptions for minority religious practices help to reform the nation's laws and institutions and as these features of the nation become more inclusive so, by definition, does its identity. Such laws and institutions over time help to shape people's sense of what the nation is, as do education systems, hence multicultural education shows children how different groups comprise the nation, shape its history and nature, and call it 'home'. Where a nation's identity and people's sense of it helps a society to be united enough to welcome and not subdue their differences, policies of multiculturalism help to include cultural minorities in both.

Post-reading Activities

Worksheet National Identity IV

Tasks:

1. What is this project about?
2. What does it achieve?

Extract: Helping young people discover their own 'British' history
www.politics.co.uk, 2 November 2012

Schools can promote social inclusion by helping children to discover a version of British history that acknowledges how people from a range of ethnic backgrounds have contributed to contemporary British society, according to new research.

A joint project between the London School of Economics, Cambridge University, Manchester University and the Runnymede Trust, Britain's leading race equality think tank, found that children from all backgrounds become more engaged with history when they are encouraged to do hands-on primary research into their own families and communities. The researchers will be sharing their findings at a seminar in November, as part of the Economic and Social Research Council (ESRC) Festival of Social Science.

The project involved over 120 young people, aged 11–14, from four schools in Cardiff, Leicester and Sheffield. Researchers worked with the students and their teachers, showing them how to use social and historical research methods, such as archive searches and oral history interviews, to explore family, community and local histories.

The students used a range of media to present the results of their research, from poetry to visual art pieces to short films and newspaper articles.

"The evaluation work we did with the students after the project showed that many of them had previously felt history was all about 'dead people'" says Dr. Claire Alexander, Professor of Sociology at Manchester University. "Performing their own primary research really made them realise that history is happening today, all around them, and they and their families are a part of it."

The project also involved young people from a wide range of ethnic backgrounds, including Bangladesh, Zambia, Somalia, Ghana, Egypt and Iraq. "People from these communities have life stories that are central to British history, but they do not get told in the history curriculum or they are only featured in a very narrow way," says Dr Alexander.

The Government's interest in what it means to be British and what kind of history is taught in schools makes the project particularly timely, says Dr Alexander.

"If you want people to have a sense of belonging, you need to present a story of 'Britishness' in which everyone can belong, where their histories and those of their families are not erased, or added in a peripheral sense. This project is about telling a different story of 'Britishness', helping young people to explore what they and their families have brought to those stories, and encouraging those from other backgrounds to recognise that these histories have a significant contribution to 'Britishness'."

Post-reading Activities

Worksheet National Identity V

Tasks:

1. Outline the content of the text and point out the author's intention.
2. In which points do you agree or disagree with the author?
3. In the context of professionalisation of mosques, discuss the German government's decision to establish the degree programme "Islamic Studies" at Tübingen University, starting in 2011, which will turn out imams for mosques in Germany.

Text: **The Challenge for us all**
Leader, The Guardian, Aug. 12, 2006

The scale and the ruthlessness of the alleged plot[22] by a group of young British Muslims to blow up passenger planes makes it inevitable that questions about the role and responsibility of Muslim communities will again be raised. John Reid, the home secretary, was right to say yesterday that terrorism threatens us all equally, and, by implication, that we all have an equal responsibility if not only practical but intellectual, because the framework for effective decisions can only be provided by agreement on the historical processes which have led to the emergence of radically disaffected Muslim youth.
This is a sad drama of impoverishment in which a significant number of young people became alienated from the culture their parents and grandparents brought to Britain without acquiring either sense of ownership in British life or a command of the broader Islamic culture which could have been theirs under other circumstances. The flux of settlement that sees an early generation assiduously protecting their culture, a second rebelling against their parents and a third moving on, has been interrupted. The collapse of the industries in which the first-comers had found work, and discrimination and ignorance on the part of the host society played a major part in the creation of this limbo, as did short-sighted, protectionist and socially regressive impulses within some of their communities. Some young men then find a way out in a second-hand form of Islam that is formulaic, generalised and organised around the principles of confrontation and resistance. A few converts from other backgrounds may then follow them, for disaffection is obviously not a solely Muslim phenomenon.

One way of responding is through the professionalisation of the mosques, so that they are served by leaders who can speak to the young in a language they understand – which is English – and widen debate within the congregation. Another is represented by the work of a new array of Muslim thinktanks and action committees. Both show the community itself embracing change. Other initiatives include the incorporation into the school curriculum of the neglected history of British Muslims before 1945, to give young Muslims and non-Muslims alike a sense that Muslims have deep roots in this country. There is a whole range of worthwhile projects, coming from all sides – but they will all take time to exercise a benign influence. The same is true of that often repeated prescription for improvements, the demand for altered foreign policies. Shifts of the kind envisaged in international life cannot simply be conjured into being to solve problems at home, however dangerous. In any case, they can take years to complete.

22 In this 2006 plot, a group of Muslim youth prepared to smuggle explosives onto planes

The need for more immediate measures is obvious. But the self-policing often demanded by outsiders rests on unrealistic ideas about the degree of social control within Muslim communities – although Muslims should be expected to do their duty as citizens if they have knowledge that crimes are being prepared. A more active approach, of the kind favoured by intellectuals such as the sociologist Tahir Abbas, would see task forces dispatched to areas where Muslims are concentrated, with resources at their disposal and a brief[23] to open up community life, air questions on Britishness, gender, arranged marriages and the Sunni-Shia relationship, organise thorough debate on foreign policy, and focus on unemployment and discrimination. It is an idea worth serious consideration.

http://www.guardian.co.uk/terrorism/story/0,,1842926,00.html

For the teacher:

Outline of the text **The Challenge for us all**

1st paragraph: Introduction:
- look at the present situation
- why radical Muslims can be found

2nd paragraph: main part a):
- looking at the past
- what went wrong
- reasons for alienation and dissatisfaction of young people

3rd paragraph: main part b):
- outlook
- possible changes for the future are suggested

4th paragraph: conclusion:
- one example of possible changes (self-policing and neighbourhood task force)

The author's intention is to raise awareness of the problem, to evoke understanding and to point out solutions.

23 brief: here: plan

Post-reading Activities

Worksheet Hanif Kureishi – Being a Writer

Tasks:

1. Watch the interview and takes notes of what Hanif Kureishi says about his career, what motivated him to become a writer.
2. Why was escaping the suburbs so important to him?
3. Compare his statements in the interview with what he writes in ***The Rainbow Sign*** (pp. 79–80).

Hanif Kureishi: 'Being a writer was like playing'

http://www.guardian.co.uk/books/video/2010/may/05/hanif-kureishi

As Hanif Kureishi publishes his collected short stories, he talks to Sarfraz Manzoor about his career, and his determination to escape the suburbs in favour of velvet trousers, drugs and cultural self-invention.

Length: 9min 23sec
Wednesday 5 May 2010

Transcript/Extract:

HK: Becoming a writer was like having a second identity. If you are living in a place where to other people you are a Paki, you are an immigrant, you are a generic disturber of the white homogeneous environment, then deciding you are a writer is like a form of assertion. 'Actually, I am not just a Paki on the street who you can spit on, I'm a writer.'

I remember thinking when I was writing in my teens, I want people to know what it's like when people go on you and call you a Paki. So this writing is a source of information about what's it like to be in Britain today. And that was one of my functions, I felt, you know, I had a place to speak, to say these things.

I think the period that I've lived through since the 1950s is absolutely fascinating. I mean, when I was a kid it was white Britain. And now it's ... you are lucky, or indeed unlucky, if you find a white person.

SM: I guess there weren't many role models for you when you were growing up, in terms of people who were from your background and your heritage who were writers.

HK: That's are absolutely true. In those days there were no real Indian writers who were at the centre of the British literary scene. There were obviously writers like Narayan and so on, you know, proper writers, but they weren't ... erm ... Forster. The only writer I guess who was significant and important was Naipaul, who had come a long way and achieved a lot. But as you say, otherwise there wasn't much going on.

Post-reading Activities

Worksheet Hanif Kureishi – Identity

Tasks:

1. What does Hanif Kureishi say about his identity and Britishness in these three extracts?
2. Compare it with what Shahid states in Kureishi's play ***Black Album***. (Extract 4)

Extract 1: Child
Hanif Kureishi, ***The Rainbow Sign***, 1986

I was born in London of an English mother and Pakistani father. My father, who lives in London, came to England from Bombay in 1947 to be educated by the old colonial power. He married here and never went back to India. The rest of his large family, his brothers, their wives, his sisters, moved from Bombay to Karachi, in Pakistan, after partition.
Frequently during my childhood, I met my Pakistani uncles when they came to London on business. They were important, confident people who took me to hotels, restaurants and Test matches, often in taxis. But I had no idea of what the subcontinent was like or how my numerous uncles, aunts and cousins lived there. When I was nine or ten a teacher purposefully placed some pictures of Indian peasants in mud huts in front of me and said to the class: Hanif comes from India. I wondered: did my uncles ride on camels? Surely not in their suits? Did my cousins, so like me in other ways, squat down in the sand like little Mowglis, half-naked and eating with their fingers?
In the mid-1960s, Pakistanis were a risible subject in England, derided on television and exploited by politicians. They had the worst jobs, they were uncomfortable in England, some of them had difficulties with the language. They were despised and out of place.
From the start I tried to deny my Pakistani self. I was ashamed. It was a curse and I wanted to be rid of it. I wanted to be like everyone else.

Extract 2: Teen
Hanif Kureishi, ***The Rainbow Sign***, 1986

Parents of my friends, both lower-middle-class and working-class, often told me they were Powell[24] supporters. Sometimes I heard them talking, heatedly, violently, about race, about 'the Pakis'. I was desperately embarrassed and afraid of being identified with these loathed aliens. I found it almost impossible to answer questions about where I came from. The word 'Pakistani' had been made into an insult. It was a word I didn't want used about myself. I couldn't tolerate being myself.
The British complained incessantly that the Pakistanis wouldn't assimilate. This meant they wanted the Pakistanis to be exactly like them. But of course even then they would have rejected them.
The British were doing the assimilating: they assimilated Pakistanis to their world view. They saw them as dirty, ignorant and less than human – worthy of abuse and violence.
At this time I found it difficult to get along with anyone. I was frightened and hostile. I suspected that my white friends were capable of racist insults. And many of them did taunt me, innocently. I reckoned

---
24 Enoch Powell, right-wing politician, racist 'Rivers of Blood' Speech, 1968

that at least once every day since I was five years old I had been racially abused. I became incapable of distinguishing between remarks that were genuinely intended to hurt and those intended as 'humour'. I became cold and distant. I began to feel I was very violent. But I didn't know how to be violent. If I had known, if that had come naturally to me, or if there'd been others I could follow, I would have made my constant fantasies of revenge into realities, I would have got into trouble, willingly hurt people, or set fire to things.

Extract 3: Man

Hanif Kureishi, ***The Rainbow Sign***, 1986

This is difficult to say. 'My country' isn't a notion that comes easily. …

Tolerant, gentle British whites[25] have no idea how little of this tolerance is experienced by blacks here. No idea of the violence, hostility and contempt directed against black people every day by state and individual alike.
It must be made clear that blacks don't require 'tolerance' in this particular condescending way. It isn't this particular paternal tyranny that is wanted, since it is major adjustments to British society that have to be made.
I stress that it is the British who have to make these adjustments.
It is the British, the white British, who have to learn that being British isn't what it was. Now it is a more complex thing, involving new elements. So there must be a fresh way of seeing Britain and the choices it faces: and a new way of being British after all this time. Much thought, discussion and self-examination must go into seeing the necessity for this, what this 'new way of being British' involves and how difficult it might be to attain.

Extract 4: I wanted to be …

Hanif Kureishi, ***Black Album***, Act One, Scene 2

Shahid, a student with Pakistani roots, tells his new-found friends Riaz and Chad that, after his father's death, he lived aimlessly.

Shahid:	I lost it for a while. Did badly at school. I'd, uh, got my girlfriend pregnant, and she'd had to have a late abortion. I started hitting the clubs, just bumming around. I couldn't concentrate on anything. I wanted – wanted to – uh –
Riaz:	Yes, yes?
Shahid:	I wanted to be a racist.
Chad:	What kind of thing are we talking about here?
Shahid:	Going around abusing Pakis, niggers, Chinks, Irish, any foreign scum. Slag them under my breath. Kick them up the arse.
Riaz:	Open your heart.
Shahid:	The thought of sleeping with Asian girls made me sick. I wouldn't touch brown flesh, except with a branding iron. Even when they came on to me, I couldn't bear it. I thought, you know, wink at an Asian girl and she'll want to marry you up.

25 George Orwell, in his 1941 essay 'England Your England' says: "the gentleness of the English civilisation is perhaps its most marked characteristic". Hanif Kureishi alludes to this statement.